I0007322

Building a Representative Theater Corpus

Angus Grieve-Smith

Building a Representative Theater Corpus

A Broader View of Nineteenth-Century French

Angus Grieve-Smith
The New School
New York, NY, USA

ISBN 978-3-030-32401-8   ISBN 978-3-030-32402-5   (eBook)
https://doi.org/10.1007/978-3-030-32402-5

© The Editor(s) (if applicable) and The Author(s) 2019
This work is subject to copyright. All rights are solely and exclusively licensed by the
Publisher, whether the whole or part of the material is concerned, specifically the rights of
translation, reprinting, reuse of illustrations, recitation, broadcasting, reproduction on
microfilms or in any other physical way, and transmission or information storage and retrieval,
electronic adaptation, computer software, or by similar or dissimilar methodology now
known or hereafter developed.
The use of general descriptive names, registered names, trademarks, service marks, etc. in this
publication does not imply, even in the absence of a specific statement, that such names are
exempt from the relevant protective laws and regulations and therefore free for general use.
The publisher, the authors and the editors are safe to assume that the advice and information
in this book are believed to be true and accurate at the date of publication. Neither the
publisher nor the authors or the editors give a warranty, express or implied, with respect to
the material contained herein or for any errors or omissions that may have been made.
The publisher remains neutral with regard to jurisdictional claims in published maps and
institutional affiliations.

Cover illustration: Pattern © Melisa Hasan

This Palgrave Pivot imprint is published by the registered company Springer Nature
Switzerland AG.
The registered company address is: Gewerbestrasse 11, 6330 Cham, Switzerland

To Charles Beaumont Wicks and all the other tool-builders.

PREFACE

THE GOAL OF THIS BOOK

Usage-based linguistics has produced a number of striking results over the years. But all these results are derived from corpora that are not representative of most speech, or even consistently representative of a single genre balance over time. Could these results be illusory? What if the patterns we have found are only artifacts of these unrepresentative corpora?

If we can find the same patterns in consistent, representative corpora, it will put these theories on firmer ground. To do this for my work on syntactic changes in French, I have created the first part of the Digital Parisian Stage corpus, a new, representative, consistent corpus of theatrical texts. Earlier studies showed that in the nineteenth century there was quite a bit of variation in the expression of negation and the use of dislocation, as a result of ongoing changes in these systems. When we compare these features in the Digital Parisian Stage with an older corpus like FRANTEXT, we find that the newer forms are more frequent in the Digital Parisian Stage, while the plays in FRANTEXT favor more conservative forms.

These differences highlight problems with the design of FRANTEXT, in particular with the "Principle of Authority" used to select texts for inclusion in the corpus. In deferring to the authority of literary historians, the architects of FRANTEXT focused the corpus on canonical texts written by and for the upper classes, pushing popular texts to the background.

Our theories of language change do not assume that language users confine their input to canonical texts, and to properly test them, we need a corpus that represents their input as closely as possible. We can never know the exact language input for a particular author from the past, and we can never create an exact sample of it, but we can do better than the Principle of Authority.

My goal with this project is to provide a workable example of representative corpus design. The compilers of the original *Trésor de la langue française* corpus abandoned the idea of representative sampling because it was beyond the resources (computing, staff and time) they had available in the 1960s. Fifty years later this is no longer the case.

The Digital Parisian Stage is largely a one-person, part-time project, conducted in New York. This is possible because it builds on several earlier projects, such as Charles Beaumont Wicks's original *The Parisian Stage* catalog, Google Books, the Gallica project of the Bibliothèque Nationale Française, the University of Warwick's Marandet collection and dezede. com. Google Books and Gallica in particular are truly massive projects, with the support of venture capitalists and national governments. Without them the project would have required a lot more visits to libraries and archives, and multiple transcontinental flights.

With these online resources, the biggest expense has been the consumer-grade personal computers that I have used to compile, OCR and clean the corpus. The other expenses—web hosting and a used copy of *The Parisian Stage*—have been minimal. A single researcher working full time with similar resources could complete a corpus like this in a relatively short period of time.

Without *The Parisian Stage* this project would have been impossible. *The Parisian Stage* itself was a life's work for Beaumont Wicks, so what can you do if you don't have a catalog like that as the basis for your project? With today's resources even that project would be quicker and easier. Many of the source texts that Wicks drew from are also available for free in Gallica and Google Books. Many historians and digital humanists are at work compiling their own exhaustive catalogs of texts, potentially available for sampling.

I hope that this book, and the project it describes, will inspire linguists and digital humanists to take the time to create representative corpora for their studies.

Some Thanks

The Digital Parisian Stage corpus and this book about it are the culmination of several ideas that have been put in my head by great teachers over the years. I found them, or they found me, at the right times, and my work is much richer for the wisdom they have passed on to me.

Don Fried suggested I write my high school English term paper on the plays of Kaufman and Hart and helped us to get the jokes in *A Midsummer Night's Dream*. He taught me that funny writing from the past can be a legitimate object of literary study.

François Némo and Mark Olsen invited me into the ARTFL project and showed me the glory of FRANTEXT. This book is partly about the flaws in that corpus, but mostly about its great achievement and its enormous potential.

Joan Bybee taught me that putting together two infamously dry fields—quantitative statistics and historical linguistics—can produce something exciting. My dissertation, *The Spread of Change in French Negation*, grew out of a term paper for her course in Frequency Effects in Language Change, and this project in turn grew out of my dissertation study.

Candace Schau taught me about representative sampling, Student's *t*-test and so much more. Her commitment to clarity and understanding built a strong foundation of statistical knowledge in my brain that has helped me withstand noise about statistics from all directions.

David Lee inspired me to think about representativeness in corpus design. Over one lunch at the Red Hawk Diner at Montclair State, he laid out a whole series of challenges to representativeness and indicated some paths forward.

Alex Gil has shown me ways to make corpora last for the future: make them light, accessible, distributed and free. In numerous presentations, workshops, commentaries, articles, tweets and conversations in the New York City Digital Humanities community, he has unapologetically pushed his agenda of equity and sustainability.

The Digital Parisian Stage project brings together Don's appreciation of non-canonical texts, François and Mark's introduction to ARTFL, Joan's use of corpora, Dr. Schau's humility in representing knowledge, David's concern for representativeness and Alex's minimalism. Without any one of these threads, this project would be much weaker.

New York, NY   Angus Grieve-Smith

CONTENTS

List of Figures

LIST OF TABLES

CHAPTER 1

Introduction

Abstract The Digital Parisian Stage project has begun with a random sample of theatrical texts from 1800 to 1815. It is intended as a consistent, representative sample of the theatrical genre for studying language change and an improvement over unrepresentative corpora like FRANTEXT, with results that can be generalized to all of Parisian theater and possibly beyond. To determine how different the Digital Parisian Stage is from FRANTEXT, Grieve-Smith compared the theatrical texts in both corpora from 1800 to 1815 on two frequency measures: declarative sentence negation and left/right dislocation. He found significant differences between the two corpora in all measures. This suggests that the results many linguists have gotten from FRANTEXT may not be accurate, and that the Digital Parisian Stage will be valuable for revising those results.

Keywords Corpus; Representative sample; French; Theater; Negation; Left dislocation; Right dislocation

The Digital Parisian Stage project aims to compile a corpus of plays that will be representative of performances in the theaters of Paris throughout history. The first section has been completed with a random sample of theatrical texts from the period 1800 through 1815, based on the list compiled by Charles Beaumont Wicks (1950), and retrieved from archives. This sampling technique goes beyond the "Principle of Authority" used for the FRANTEXT corpus, to include playwrights and characters from a wider range of social backgrounds, giving a very different picture of the language. To confirm this broader representation I conducted studies of two groups of morphosyntactic features known to vary with social class: declarative sentence negation and dislocation constructions.

To begin with, a note on the concept of "corpus." The word means "body" in Latin, and is typically used to refer to a group of texts that constitute a body in the sense of being a coherent whole, although sometimes this coherence can be more imagined and aspirational than real. Corpora have been created and used for hundreds of years, sometimes to study the work of a single author, sometimes of a group of authors, sometimes of a literary canon. The use of the phrases *corpus iuris* and *corpus canonum* to refer to a collection of legal texts dates back to the twelfth century (Van Hove 1908). Later corpora were used to group literary texts together for easy reference when writing criticism; Chambers (1728) notes: "We have also a corpus of the Greek poets; and another of the Latin poets."

Linguists and lexicographers have been compiling digital corpora for analytical papers and dictionaries since the mid-twentieth century. After W. Nelson Francis and Henry Kučera created the Brown Corpus of English (1964), Houghton-Mifflin licensed it as the basis for the *American Heritage Dictionary* (1969). FRANTEXT was compiled in the 1960s with the goal of creating a new dictionary, the *Trésor de la langue française* (Imbs 1971). Since that time, other, larger corpora have been created, but FRANTEXT has been the reference corpus for historical studies of the French language.

These corpora are particularly useful for testing diachronic predictions from usage-based linguistic theories, such as the effect of type frequency on linguistic productivity (Bybee 1995). Imagine a French adolescent in the seventeenth century forgetting which negation construction typically goes with the verb *cesser* and picking the one that seems to go with lots of verbs. This is the type of mechanism assumed by the theory of type frequency.

In order to properly test these theories, however, we need something resembling the language of the past. We have no access to the spontaneous conversations of seventeenth-century adolescents, but instead we can imagine a playwright composing dialogue and verse, reaching into his or her memory for appropriate models. Some of these playwrights may have only looked to earlier playwrights, but others paid attention to the language they heard from their friends, from their servants and on the street.

We have many plays from the past, but we cannot analyze them all at the level we need to test these theories, and they are not all interchangeable. We need a representative sample.

FRANTEXT may have been appropriate for the construction of a dictionary marketed to "the cultivated man" (Imbs 1971: XVIII), but the Principle of Authority introduces a strong bias in favor of elite theater. The Digital Parisian Stage, based on a random sample of all plays that premièred in Paris in the nineteenth century, aims to rectify that bias, offering a broader view of the language of this period that in turn produces more reliable studies of language change.

To compare the Digital Parisian Stage against FRANTEXT, I annotated 22 plays from the Digital Parisian Stage corpus for dislocation and negation features and compared them to the four plays chosen for the FRANTEXT corpus for this period, with striking results. In the Digital Parisian Stage plays, 74% of declarative sentence negations used *ne … pas*, while in the FRANTEXT plays it was only 50% ($p < 0.001$).

I chose negation constructions because the study I conducted for my dissertation, *The Spread of Change in French Negation* (Grieve-Smith 2009), investigated change in negation in the theatrical texts in FRANTEXT. In that study I found that the increase in frequency of *ne … pas* from the sixteenth through twentieth centuries fit the predictions of Kroch's (1989) logistic model, and that the logistic model in turn could be explained by the theory of type frequency.

I also looked at left and right dislocation constructions, building on a study where I found a general increase in those constructions in the late twentieth century (Grieve-Smith 2000). For left dislocation constructions, 0.760% of non-interrogative sentences used the contrastive topic construction in the Digital Parisian Stage plays, compared to 0.238% in the FRANTEXT plays ($p < 0.05$, $d = 1.04$), and 0.113% of non-interrogative sentences (19) used the demonstrative left dislocation (CLD) construction, compared to just one token in FRANTEXT (0.00903%, $d = 0.595$). The difference in clitic right dislocations was extreme (0.420% for the Digital Parisian Stage plays but only 0.0918% in the FRANTEXT plays, $p < 0.01$, $d = 1.13$).

At least one of these differences can be shown to be due to the bias introduced by the Principle of Authority used to compile FRANTEXT. The Digital Parisian Stage corpus contains plays from 9 genres and 11 theaters, while the 4 plays from FRANTEXT are drawn from 3 genres and only 2 theaters, plus 1 closet play. The relative token frequency of *ne* alone is associated with both the genre of the play and the theater where it was performed, and *ne ... pas* is associated with genre (one-way ANOVA, $p < 0.05$).

Several of the other negation and dislocation constructions displayed potential associations between corpus and theater, genre or some of the characteristics of the characters (age, gender and social class). None of these were strong enough to rule out the possibility of sampling error given the size of the sample, but they suggest that once more data is collected for the Digital Parisian Stage corpus, either in the Napoleonic period or later in the nineteenth century, the possibility of sampling error for those factors may be within the typically acceptable range ($\alpha = 0.05$).

These findings are specific to a short period, 1800–1815, and as such they do not have any immediate bearing on diachronic studies like my dissertation on negation (Grieve-Smith 2009) or my study on dislocation (Grieve-Smith 2000). They do suggest that when the 1% sample is complete for the entire nineteenth century, we will see patterns that are similar, but drawn from a more reliable sample that is likely to be closer to informal spontaneous conversation.

It is my hope that these findings will encourage more people to contribute to the Digital Parisian Stage project. For those whose area of focus does not include nineteenth-century Parisian French, I hope this report will encourage them to design and contribute to similarly representative projects in their areas. This will likely include the type of work contributed by Wicks (1950 et seq.), compiling records of language production into a comprehensive catalog that can serve as the sampling frame for a new corpus.

REFERENCES

American Heritage Dictionary. 1969. Boston: Houghton Mifflin.

Bybee, Joan. 1995. Regular Morphology and the Lexicon. *Language and Cognitive Processes* 10: 425–455.

Chambers, Ephraim. 1728. Corpus. In *Cyclopædia*. London: Chambers.

Francis, W. Nelson, and Henry Kučera. 1964. *A Standard Corpus of Present-Day Edited American English, for Use with Digital Computers*. Providence: Brown.

Grieve-Smith, Angus. 2000. Topicalization and Word Order in Conversational French. Southeastern Conference on Linguistics, Oxford, Mississippi.

———. 2009. *The Spread of Change in French Negation*. Ph.D. diss., University of New Mexico.

Imbs, Paul. 1971. Préface. In *Trésor de la langue française*. Paris: Editions du Centre National de la Recherche Scientifique.

Kroch, Anthony. 1989. Reflexes of Grammar in Patterns of Language Change. *Language Variation and Change* 1: 199–244.

Van Hove, Alphonse. 1908. Corpus Juris Canonici. In *The Catholic Encyclopedia*. New York: Robert Appleton Company.

Wicks, Charles Beaumont. 1950. *The Parisian Stage*. Tuscaloosa: University of Alabama.

CHAPTER 2

Capturing Language Diversity Through Representative Samples

Abstract Usage-based theories of language, such as reduction, reanalysis, analogical extension, propagation and entrenchment, offer explanations of the state of a language at one point in time based on the ways it was used in a prior point in time. We can test these theoretical constructs with representative samples, following Laplace's (*Essai philosophique sur les probabilités.* Paris: Courcier, 1814) estimate of the population of the French Empire. Laplace's methods can be misapplied in numerous ways, particularly by choosing a biased sample or by sampling from an inapplicable frame. An ideal corpus would have a balance of genres that matches the input that authors experience, and a corpus of theater is an initial step toward that ideal.

Keywords Usage-based; Sampling; Hypothesis testing; Genre

My purpose in compiling the Digital Parisian Stage is to investigate why and how languages change. I am particularly interested in usage-based theories of change involving phonological reduction, reanalysis, analogical extension, propagation and entrenchment. The technique I describe in this book is focused on the use of representative corpora to investigate these theories, but the principles of representative sampling are essential to investigating many claims of linguistic theory.

© The Author(s) 2019
A. Grieve-Smith, *Building a Representative Theater Corpus*,
https://doi.org/10.1007/978-3-030-32402-5_2

Science builds on both existential and universal observations, and the science of language is no exception. To justify a simple existential statement like "a French playwright negated a sentence with *pas* alone and no *ne* in the nineteenth century," we only need one reliable observation. To be completely sure of a universal statement like "all of the negative sentences in this play were negated with *ne … pas*," we need to have observed all of the negative sentences. Average statements, like "the mean length of plays in this decade was three hundred lines," and fractional statements, like "thirty-five percent of the negated sentences in this play were negated with *ne … pas*," are also universal statements, because for complete confidence in the percentage they require us to observe all of the plays, or all of the negated sentences.

2.1   Usage-Based Theories of Language Change

In these usage-based theories, the changes in question are triggered or conditioned by the state of the language at the time. Specifically, they posit that a language user produces a given word (or construction) because of their memory of perceiving and producing that word and related words.

Linguists (e.g., Sturtevant 1917: 68; Wang 1969) have long observed that certain sound changes are found in some lexical items years before they are found in other lexical items. Joan Bybee (Hooper 1976) noted that in those changes, more frequent lexical items tend to display the change earlier than less frequent items. The usage-based explanation for this (Bybee and Thompson 1997) is that people produce a reduced form of a word or phrase because they have produced it many times before and want to save time and effort.

Reanalysis is the process whereby language users at one point in time perceive a sequence of language as having a different structure than users of the same language did at an earlier point in time; see Croft (2000: chapter 5) for an in-depth discussion of various types of reanalysis. It is important to note that our evidence of reanalysis is almost always indirect. We rarely, if ever, have psycholinguistic evidence of the structures that language users have perceived in a given sequence at two points in time on a historic scale. Instead, we observe that at one point the sequence is used in a way that is consistent with structure A and inconsistent with structure B, and at a later point it is used in a way that is inconsistent with structure A and consistent with structure B. As Traugott (1989) observed, there will almost always be uses that are consistent with both structures during this period.

Croft's First Law of Propagation (2000: 176) states that over the long term, situations where a single community uses two different variants to fulfill the same function are unstable, and language users tend to eliminate that overlap. This can happen in one of three ways: the first is that the alternative forms can be reassigned to different functions so that they are no longer in competition. The second is that the variation can be reinterpreted as corresponding to a division of the community. The third is to gradually shift the community toward the use of one variant or the other.

When this kind of propagation happens, there is typically an entrenched legacy pattern that reflects the earlier usage. This pattern tends to remain in individual forms based on their per-word token frequency. As Bybee and Thompson (1997: 379) write, "this conserving effect is related to the faster lexical access of high frequency forms: the more a form is used, the more its representation is strengthened, making it easier to access the next time. Words that are strong in memory and easy to access are not likely to be replaced by new forms created with the regular pattern."

2.2   Testing Usage-Based Theories

By definition, usage-based theories predict a correlation between the forms that a language user produces at a given point in time and the forms that they have perceived and produced in their lifetime up to that point. Testing these predictions requires us to have good data not only about what forms a language user produces at one point in time but also about what that user might have heard, said, seen, signed or written at previous points in time. These are universal statements: they describe all of the tokens of a particular linguistic form that a language user produces in a given time frame (or text) and all the tokens that they have perceived in the time preceding that production.

Most of the articles and books articulating these usage-based theories base them on unrepresentative examples, many of them collected ad hoc and not taken from planned corpora. The hypotheses generated by these theories could benefit from more rigorous, quantitative corpus testing. This was the idea behind the study in my dissertation, *The Spread of Change in French Negation* (Grieve-Smith 2009).

In the Spread of Change study I found evidence for all the processes mentioned above (reduction, extension, reanalysis, propagation and entrenchment) in sentence negation in French—essentially, in the change from *ne* alone to *ne … pas* and *ne … point*—in a corpus of theatrical texts drawn from FRANTEXT. These were promising results, but I was concerned that the corpus was not representative enough to give me an idea of what the playwrights in question had really read and heard in the past, and thus to justify making universal statements about that variety of language.

This was the impetus for the Digital Parisian Stage project. The goal is to put usage-based theories on a firmer footing by providing a representative sample of French spanning the nineteenth century. In the next section I will discuss the importance of representativeness in sampling and some techniques for representative sampling.

2.3   SAMPLING IN POPULATION STUDIES

The sampling techniques I use in this book come from the field of population studies, which in turn based them on strategies developed for gambling. The Marquis de Laplace noted (coincidentally, in the early nineteenth century, 1814: 45), that the French Empire did not have reliable population counts for the territory it controlled, although it had reliable birth records for every municipality. He argued based on numerous case studies that the ratio of total population to birth rate was relatively constant across Europe, so that if the government had an estimate of that ratio it could multiply that by the recorded birth rates to estimate the total population size.

Laplace then reasoned that the government could estimate the average birth rate by "choosing districts distributed in a roughly uniform manner throughout the Empire, in order to generalize the result, independently of local circumstances." He based his method on the Law of Large Numbers discovered by Jacob Bernoulli (1713), which asserts that the outcome of repeated executions of random events, such as spins of a roulette wheel, will tend to converge on the expected value of the events. Sampling the population size in a random district is exactly the kind of event that Bernoulli described (a Bernoulli trial), and that measuring the population size (and then determining the ratio of population to birth rate in a large enough number of samples) would therefore yield an average that approached the average throughout the Empire.

In 1802, based on Laplace's recommendations, the then-French Republic conducted a population count of 30 out of its 108 districts, yielding an average ratio of 28.352843 inhabitants per annual birth. He used this to estimate the total population of all 108 districts at 42,529,627, with a 1 in 1161 chance that the error was greater than half a million people (1.17% of the total). Laplace did not have a reliable census count to compare his estimate with, but his methods have been confirmed by years of follow-up research. They have also been applied beyond the field of population studies, including biology, medicine and agriculture (Student 1908: 22).

Laplace recommended this method because a full population census is "arduous and difficult to conduct accurately." This is an important fact to keep in mind in all discussions of sampling. Sampling is a labor-saving device, reducing the number of observations required to reach a conclusion with an acceptable level of accuracy.

The numerous tests of statistical significance developed by Student (1908) and others are all based on Laplace's sampling methods. They are refinements of Laplace's figure of 1 in 1161: given a measurement and a sample size, what is the probability (p) that that measurement is due to accidentally sampling unrepresentative members of the population? Is this probability within a range that is acceptable to us?

Corpus linguists often advertise how many millions of words their corpora contain; this is done partly to enable studies of rare phenomena and of correlations that may subdivide the total corpus, but it is also done partly out of a sense that bigger is always better. That sense is mistaken; as Student (1908) demonstrated, there is no absolute minimum size for a sample. The size necessary to support generalizing a difference in means is a function of that difference, the standard error of the two distributions and the amount of uncertainty about sampling error that the reader finds acceptable. As we will see in later chapters, a relatively small sample is perfectly adequate if the other measures are within the appropriate ranges.

2.4 THE SAMPLING FRAME AND THE LIMITS OF GENERALIZATION

There are several ways that Laplace's methods can be misapplied, yielding results that are inaccurate or misleading. The most problematic is to use sampling methods that are not representative, and thus likely to incorporate bias in some way, such as a researcher sending a survey invitation to their Twitter followers. Another is to sample from a frame that is not applicable to the research question. The first mistake is inherent in the design of FRANTEXT, and the second is common in the use of FRANTEXT in diachronic studies.

In Laplace's estimate of the population of France in 1802, his research question was simple: "determine the population of a great empire." The sample was the 30 districts where the government took a census count, while the total 108 districts of the then-Republic constitute the sampling frame. The research question applied directly to the sampling frame, and the uniform sampling justified generalizing the results from the sample to the entire frame.

The 108 districts of the French Republic in 1802 were well known, but in a study of language the appropriate sampling frame is not always so obvious. The Brown Corpus (Francis and Kučera 1964) was compiled on the basis of samples drawn from the Brown University Library catalog, meaning that the results of studies based on Brown can be generalized to the titles in that catalog.

These results can only be generalized to the English language as a whole to the extent that those catalogs or indices themselves are representative of the English language. This is problematic, because the Brown library catalog is not a random sample. Each of those books was published or distributed based on a series of conscious decisions made by the publishers. The catalog is further filtered by the acquisition decisions of the University librarians. These two levels of bias preclude results based on the Brown Corpus from being automatically generalized to the English language as a whole.

2.5   Sampling Frames for Language

In order to test a question like "Can changes in type frequency in one period be predicted by the type frequency in an earlier period?" we need to understand where and how to measure type frequency. We can measure the type frequency in the later period by measuring the output of language users during that period, but how do we measure the preceding period?

A language user can derive their sense of relative type frequency from the language they perceive, or from the language they produce. It is possible that both experiences are relevant, and to my knowledge this question has not yet been fully tested. Bybee's theory rested on the input (Bybee 1995: 427), so this is what I chose to test for the Spread of Change study.

This leads us to the key challenge in the design of historical corpora, where the question of bias and sampling frames intersects with language variation. Language varies according to multiple factors including region, social class, gender and situation. A corpus is likely to include the production of several individual language users, in multiple varieties, from every period. Each language user is likely to have been exposed to multiple varieties over the course of their life.

FRANTEXT contains theater, novels, poetry, short stories, letters, scientific articles and other genres. Genres of writing are known for having particular styles of language (Biber 1988). It is generally enough to read a single page of a text, without differences of formatting or topic, to know whether that text is a play, a poem, a short story or a political pamphlet.

How well do the varieties in the corpus at one period represent the varieties that the authors in a subsequent period were exposed to? There have been efforts to record the proportions of various varieties in the input of particular users, but it is obvious that historical corpora cannot reproduce these proportions well. A particular difficulty is the way that the genre balance of recorded texts changes over time. There were no tweets, IRC chat messages or telegrams before 1800, and relatively few epic poems and mystery plays after 1700.

Another difficulty is that every language user is exposed to multiple informal conversational language varieties; the bulk of language input for most speakers is in informal conversation. For any period before the widespread use of cheap voice recording, a corpus is highly unlikely to have these varieties represented in any proportion comparable to the input received by a typical language user.

There are strategies that we can use to compensate for the lack of informal conversation in our sampling frames. Other varieties share features with informal conversation, either by accident or by design. One such variety is the language of theater. Many theatrical scenes are intended as reasonable facsimiles of informal conversations.

This is not to say that theatrical scripts can be relied on as faithful reproductions of informal conversational language. They are usually planned in advance, for comedic or dramatic effect: "scripted" has even become an adjective indicating an activity that seems spontaneous on one level but was planned in detail. The scripts may leave room for actors to improvise lines, or even record lines that were improvised on stage, but even ad-libbed lines do not reliably have the same features as truly spontaneous conversation.

Theatrical language also has a tendency to develop its own conventions and formulas, different from those of formal conversation. At regular intervals in the history of theater, playwrights and directors are acclaimed for having put "real language on stage," with the implication that the rest of theatrical language was unnatural.

There is a wide range of variation within theater, including genre variation (Wicks 1950 references comedy, drama, folie, pantomime and 28 other genres). The characters represented on stage are drawn from multiple social classes, genders and regions, and they are given voices that at least aim to represent the language of those classes, genders and regions.

Unfortunately, the characters in a fiction corpus are not necessarily representative of the population that the corpus claims to present. There are several occasions where the corpus may be biased. The playwright chooses to focus on particular characters, and to represent them in particular ways. The theater management chooses plays to produce based in part on what they expect will sell tickets. The theater may be censored by the government. Publishers choose plays to publish based in part on their success at the box office. Libraries and archives choose plays to store, to reproduce and to digitize. Corpus designers choose plays to include in the corpus.

The field of corpus linguistics has long grappled with the notion of representativeness, and what is necessary for findings from a corpus to be generalized to "a language" (see Biber 1993 for a summary up to that point). It is impossible to create a representative sample of an entire language from a period before speech recording was ubiquitous. The best that historical linguists can do is to take samples of segments of a language and report their sampling methods with clarity and humility. This allows the readers to make the generalizations that they feel comfortable making.

References

Bernoulli, Jacob. 1713. *Ars conjectandi*. Basel: Thurnisiorum.

Biber, Douglas. 1988. *Variation Across Speech and Writing*. Cambridge: Cambridge University Press.

———. 1993. Representativeness in Corpus Design. *Literary and Linguistic Computing* 8 (4): 243–257.

Bybee, Joan. 1995. Regular Morphology and the Lexicon. *Language and Cognitive Processes* 10: 425–455.

Bybee, Joan, and Sandra A. Thompson. 1997. Three Frequency Effects in Syntax. *Proceedings of the Twenty-Third Annual Meeting of the Berkeley Linguistics Society: General Session and Parasession on Pragmatics and Grammatical Structure*, 378–388.

Croft, William. 2000. *Explaining Language Change: An Evolutionary Approach.* London: Longman.

Francis, W. Nelson, and Henry Kučera. 1964. *A Standard Corpus of Present-Day Edited American English, for Use with Digital Computers.* Providence: Brown.

Grieve-Smith, Angus. 2009. *The Spread of Change in French Negation.* Ph.D. diss., University of New Mexico.

Hooper, Joan B. 1976. Word Frequency in Lexical Diffusion and the Source of Morphophonological Change. In *Current Progress in Historical Linguistics*, ed. William Christie, 96–105. Amsterdam: North Holland.

de Laplace, Pierre-Simon. 1814. *Essai philosophique sur les probabilités.* Paris: Courcier.

Student. 1908. The Probable Error of a Mean. *Biometrika* 6: 1–25.

Sturtevant, E.H. 1917. *Linguistic Change: An Introduction to the Historical Study of Language.* Chicago: University of Chicago.

Traugott, Elizabeth Closs. 1989. On the Rise of Epistemic Meanings in English: An Example of Subjectification in Semantic Change. *Language* 65: 31–55.

Wang, William S.-Y. 1969. Competing Changes as a Cause of Residue. *Language* 45 (1): 9–25.

Wicks, Charles Beaumont. 1950, 1953, 1961, 1967, 1979. *The Parisian Stage.* Tuscaloosa: University of Alabama.

CHAPTER 3

FRANTEXT's Corpus of Nineteenth-Century French

Abstract FRANTEXT was first collected in the 1960s for the *Trésor de la langue française* dictionary. Due to demand from researchers it was cleaned up and released on CD-ROM and on the Internet in the 1980s and 1990s. The original intent was to base it on a representative sample, but due to time constraints it was compiled using an unrepresentative "Principle of Authority." For the period 1800–1815 the result is four texts chosen based on the subjective interests of literary historians.

Keywords French language; Nineteenth century; Dictionary; Literary history

FRANTEXT is the primary corpus of nineteenth-century French, containing 78 plays from that century. If it were representative, it could be a hugely powerful tool for investigating the French of that period. Unfortunately, as we will see later in this chapter, it is by no means a uniform sample. Another corpus, *Le Corpus de la littérature narrative du Moyen Age au XXe siècle*, produced by Classiques Garnier Numérique and the Centre National d'Enseignement à Distance, contains only narrative fiction such as novels and short stories and appears to follow a similar "Principle of Authority" to that used in FRANTEXT. For its summary the Garnier corpus provides only a list of names of well-known authors for each century. For this work I will focus on FRANTEXT.

© The Author(s) 2019
A. Grieve-Smith, *Building a Representative Theater Corpus*,
https://doi.org/10.1007/978-3-030-32402-5_3

3.1   The *Trésor de la langue française* and FRANTEXT

Compilers of dictionaries have a longstanding practice of referring to literary works for usage examples, and literary corpora are an efficient way of finding these kinds of examples, so after Francis and Kučera created the Brown Corpus (1964), Houghton-Mifflin licensed it as the basis for the *American Heritage Dictionary* (1969). Scholars at the French Centre National de la Recherche Scientifique (CNRS) were already at work on a dictionary of the French language that they hoped would rival the *Oxford English Dictionary*, and had made the decision in 1957 to "shorten the editing time through the use of machines, which will also enable us to collect a large variety of examples from numerous and varied texts" (Imbs 1971: XIV).

The corpus that the editors intended to use for this new dictionary, the *Trésor de la langue française*, was ambitious, even audacious: a representative sample of text from the seventeenth through the twentieth centuries—and speech from the twentieth century, all compiled on punch cards and paper tape. Sadly, this corpus was never created. Even with the most advanced computer produced in France, the multithreaded Bull Gamma 60, the researchers realized that it would take them years to compile and analyze such a large corpus (Imbs 1971: XXIII).

The CNRS then took a step back and considered the likely audience for their dictionary: a "cultivated man" from "the upper and middle ranks of society" who desired to produce "careful enunciations, sometimes obeying empirical norms and sometimes departing from belabored clauses" (Imbs 1971: XVIII). They got to work creating a new, slimmed down collection of language, for the basis of a product that would appeal to this cultivated man.

The authors of the dictionary chose the texts for this corpus based on a "Principle of Authority." They consulted several well-regarded literary histories of French in the nineteenth and twentieth centuries and made lists of every work mentioned in those histories. Nineteenth-century works that were mentioned five times or more and twentieth-century works that were mentioned four times or more were automatically included in the corpus. Works that were mentioned two or three times (or four times in histories of nineteenth-century literature) were discussed in committee for possible inclusion, based on criteria such as their popularity, the richness of their vocabulary and the "sûreté" (roughly, confidence) of their language.

As volumes of the dictionary appeared, the researchers became aware that there was demand by other scholars for consultation of the corpus independent of the dictionary. The Brown Corpus had inspired a host of other English corpora, such as the Lancaster-Oslo-Bergen corpus and the British National Corpus, with the result that language scholars became increasingly aware of the value of corpora. The *Trésor de la langue française* editors made an arrangement with the University of Chicago in 1982 to transfer the texts to magnetic media and make them available over the Internet. In 1989 the American and French Research on the Treasury of the French Language (ARTFL) consortium launched an Internet server that allowed affiliated researchers to retrieve concordances, per-text frequency counts and keyword in context (KWIC) citations (de Surmont 2006).

This broader audience and wider range of functions brought to light inaccuracies and cosmetic problems with the corpus that had been less of a concern when in-house researchers were compiling the dictionary, and ARTFL worked to clean up the texts. This is where I have a bit part in the story: as a graduate student at Chicago in 1993–1994, I was hired by ARTFL to proofread texts from the corpus against paper first edition copies. The concordance and frequencies were soon made available on the new World Wide Web, in the United States as ARTFL and in France as FRANTEXT.

In the ensuing years the Laboratoire de l'Analyse et traitement informatique de la langue française (ATILF), successor to the original dictionary project, has produced a CD-ROM and an online version of the dictionary. They have also made the full text of many of the works available. In this time the ARTFL project has digitized numerous works of the seventeenth and eighteenth centuries, including the original Encyclopedia first published by Diderot and d'Alembert in 1751.

3.2   THE *TRÉSOR DE LA LANGUE FRANÇAISE* AS DESCRIPTIVE ADVICE

The adoption of the Principle of Authority in the *Trésor de la langue française* may not fit well with the goals I laid out in Chap. 2 for understanding language change, so why did the CNRS use it? It makes sense in the context of what Sheidlower (1996) called "descriptive advice." Descriptive advice has a long history. It is a good description of foreign language instruction: giving travelers and immigrants advice on how to make themselves understood and avoid discrimination in an unfamiliar country. That was the value provided by the first known dictionaries and grammars of the French language like Palsgrave (1530).

In seventeenth-century France, dictionaries and grammars were put to a slightly different use. As the kings centralized their courts on Paris and then on Versailles, the speech and writing styles of the elite were centralized along with them. People who showed too much evidence of their regional or class origins found themselves targets of mockery and discrimination, often from other insecure provincials.

Some of these provincials, like François de Malherbe in his 225-page commentary on the 600-page collected works of Philippe des Portes (1606), tried to avoid arbitrary criticism, by being explicit about his own judgments of taste ("I don't like this epithet"), invoking specific principles ("Superfluous.," "Cheville."), or referring to common usage ("You must consult your ear," and "People don't say … but …").

King Louis XIII and his minister Richelieu realized that the principled approach of Malherbe could be used to create a slightly more open standard, a centralized language that would help integrate provincial courtiers into the national elite (Caillet 1857), to compete with the Spanish of Cervantes and the Italian of Dante. They created the Académie Française to adjudicate disputes over this standard and develop a dictionary, like the second-language dictionaries but aimed at native speakers of French, which was first published in complete form in 1694.

Vaugelas (1647) contributed to this enterprise and took Malherbe's admonition to "consult your ear" to a new level, creating a grammar based on the speech and writings of those who were successful at court and in other elite circles and regarded as worthy models for ambitious provincials and immigrants. Vaugelas wrote, on the first page of his Preface (page vj):

> These are not just laws I made for our language based on some personal prerogative of mine. That would be reckless, some would say insane, because what authority, what basis do I have for claiming a privilege that is the sole right of Usage—the power that everyone recognizes as the Lord and Master of modern languages?

Vaugelas's point—the reason people bought his book—was not to base these laws on all usage, but on "good usage," *le bon Vsage*, which he explicitly defined as the usage of the members of King Louis XIV's court. He elevated the usage of elites to an abstract principle and positioned himself as an authority on that usage.

Before the era of computer corpora, compiling grammars and dictionaries for descriptive advice as Vaugelas did was long, hard work. Rather than doing the work of changing their grammars to keep up with changing usage, and confronting the eternal conservatism of literary critics, many grammarians preferred to recycle the previous generations' admonitions and prohibitions. Even in the twenty-first century, some grammars promote rules that haven't been accurate since before Vaugelas and Malherbe consulted their ears. These peeves tend to accumulate over the centuries, with teachers repeating most of the rules they heard from their teachers, and only throwing out the most egregious ones. After a few centuries of this, many saw standard grammar as a meaningless burden, unconnected to the reality of effective writing.

In the twentieth century, grammarians and lexicographers were inspired by the successes of "hard sciences" like physics and biology and aimed to replicate the stance of neutral detachment cultivated by those sciences. Echoing ecological approaches to science, they portrayed language as a part of Nature, to be observed and left untouched like a mountain or a species of fish, and they strongly condemned the heavy-handed approach the grammarians took with it. In the United States they wrote books like *Leave Your Language Alone* (Hall 1950). In France they rebranded their discipline as *sciences du langage*.

This scientific approach is valuable, as there are indeed scientific questions to be answered through the study of language. Why do people speak differently in different places and circumstances? Why do people write differently depending on their purpose? How does language change? How do grammatical forms change?

This detached attitude toward language challenged the strict grammar approach but made little headway outside of academic contexts. Researchers also found that demand for pure science of language was limited, especially compared with the demand for descriptive advice. Just as there are more jobs for actuaries and accountants than for mathematicians, there have always been more jobs for language and writing teachers than for language scientists. Demand for accurate, scientifically based information about languages has been growing in recent years, but even now would it be enough to fund a corpus on the scale of FRANTEXT?

When the creators of the *Trésor de la langue française* shifted from representing the entire language to digitizing a list of works based on the Principle of Authority, it was an acknowledgment that they saw more demand from cultivated men for descriptive advice than from academics for scientific analysis. Printing and distributing an 11-volume dictionary is not cheap, to say nothing of the cost of the computer, and even the CNRS could not justify the expense on the basis of sales to researchers alone. They needed the cultivated man.

3.3   FRANTEXT's View of Theater
in the Napoleonic Period

When we follow the Principle of Authority, what do we get? By simple number of works included, FRANTEXT is by no means a uniform sample. Some authors are widely overrepresented: of a total of 78 plays in the nineteenth century (less than 0.25% of the total listed by Wicks), the corpus includes 12 plays by Théodore Leclerc, 13 by Alfred de Musset and 7 by Paul Claudel. The corpus for the period 1800–1815 contains four plays, as listed in Table 3.1:

Why those four plays? As described by Imbs (1971), they were each mentioned at least three times total in the literary histories of the nineteenth century that the lexicographers consulted. For nineteenth-century theater, the authorities were Bédier and Hazard (1948), Lanson (1912), Queneau (1958), Thibaudet (1937) and van Tieghem (1937).

Reading these literary histories, it is clear that the authorities were focused on works produced by and for wealthy elites. Thibaudet (1937) consecrates an entire chapter to the writer and philosopher Germaine de Staël, a chapter to her parents (her father was Jacques Necker, finance minister to Louis XVI), and another to her associates, including her romantic partner Benjamin Constant, 18 pages in total. Other chapters are devoted to Napoleon's taste in literature, Chateaubriand and the

Table 3.1   Theatrical texts included in FRANTEXT for the period 1800–1815

Author	Gregorian date	Republican date	Title
Constant de Rebecque, Benjamin	1809		Wallstein
Guilbert de Pixérécourt, René Charles	September 3, 1800	16 fructidor an VIII	Cœlina, ou l'enfant du mystère
Népomucène Lemercier, Louis Jean	March 22, 1800	1 germinal an VIII	Pinto, ou la Journée d'une conspiration
Legouvé, Gabriel	June 25, 1806		La Mort de Henri Quatre, Roi de France

revolutionary émigrés. None of his chapters on the early nineteenth century focus on popular theater, or any popular forms of literature.

Queneau (1958: 1112) also discusses de Staël and Constant at length, arguing that with *Wallstein* and related works they undermined conservative norms that constrained the forms of theater, without openly challenging them:

> As early as 1809, in his *Réflexions sur la tragédie de Wallenstein et sur le théâtre allemand*, Benjamin Constant exposed the doctrine of Coppet. These are cautious pages, where he does not attack classical tragedy, sets great store on the three *unités*, and refrains from proposing German theater as a model. When he adapts *Wallenstein*, he maintains the psychological complexity of the characters but introduces the *unités*. In *de l'Allemagne*, Madame de Staël adds to these principles the notion, destined for great consequences, that classical tragedy only speaks to the limited audience of the aristocracy.

Ironically, despite what de Staël and Queneau write, the language of Constant's *Wallstein* is as aristocratic and elitist as any of the other FRANTEXT plays. Bédier and Hazard (1948) also spend multiple pages discussing the work of de Staël and her associates, and other liberal challenges to theatrical norms. Here is what they write about Népomucène Lemercier's *Pinto* (page 183):

> In his *Pinto* (1800) he executes an original idea: in telling of a tragic conspiracy that will liberate Portugal from Spanish domination, the one who pulls all the strings in the plot, stokes everyone's courage, moves aside obstacles that appear at the last minute, takes action and in the end triumphs—is a valet, it is Pinto: Pinto is the ancestor of Ruy Blas, if you will. But when all is said and done, Népomucène Lemercier remains an aborted talent.

In point of fact, Pinto is not a valet but a secretary to Duke João of Braganza, with significantly more education and power than a valet. As is common with employees of the uppermost classes, his speech is much closer to his superiors in the play, and to other nobles and royals on the French theater, than to the speech of servants working for characters who are bourgeois or small rural landowners.

As I discussed in Chap. 2, the available archive of plays reflects the biases of the playwrights, theater managers, government censors, publishers, audiences, librarians, archivists and corpus designers. The Principle of Authority used in selecting texts for FRANTEXT introduced another source of bias: the authors and publishers of the literary histories consulted. Not only were these authors biased by virtue of their social class and education, but the goals of these literary histories were to inform critics and writers about interesting developments in the literary canon, not to represent the full range of works produced during that period.

REFERENCES

American Heritage Dictionary. 1969. Boston: Houghton Mifflin.

Bédier, Joseph, and Paul Hazard. 1948. *Littérature française*. Paris: Larousse.

Caillet, Jules. 1857. *De l'administration en France sous le ministère du cardinal de Richelieu*. Paris: Firmin Didot Frères.

Francis, W. Nelson, and Henry Kučera. 1964. *A Standard Corpus of Present-Day Edited American English, for Use with Digital Computers*. Providence: Brown.

Hall, Robert A. 1950. *Leave Your Language Alone*. Ithaca: Linguistica.

Imbs, Paul. 1971. *Trésor de la langue française*. Paris: CNRS.

Lanson, Gustave. 1912. *Manuel bibliographique de la littérature française moderne 1500–1900*. Paris: Hachette.

de Malherbe, François. 1606. *Commentaire sur des Portes*. *Œuvres complètes*, 249–474. Paris: Hachette.

Palsgrave, John. 1530. *L'Eclaircissement de la langue française*. Paris: Génin.

Queneau, Raymond. 1958. *Littératures françaises, connexes et marginales. Histoire des littératures, v. 3*. Paris: Gallimard.

Sheidlower, Jesse. 1996. Elegant Variations and All That. *The Atlantic*.

Surmont, Jean-Nicolas de. (2006). De la genèse à l'informatisation du Trésor de la langue française et du Grand Robert électronique. *Revista De Filología Románica* 23: 55–66.

Thibaudet, Albert. 1937. *Histoire de la littérature française de 1789 a nos jours*. Paris: Stock.

van Tieghem, Paul. 1937. *Répertoire chronologique des littératures modernes*. Paris: Droz.

de Vaugelas, Claude Favre. 1647. *Remarques sur la langue françoise*. Paris: Augustin Courbe.

CHAPTER 4

The Digital Parisian Stage Project

Abstract In the early nineteenth century Paris hosted a wide variety of theaters, even after Napoleon reduced their number in 1807. Charles Beaumont Wicks's exhaustive catalog of plays that premièred in Paris in the nineteenth century is an ideal sampling frame for a new corpus. The Digital Parisian Stage corpus is based on a random 1% sample of the plays listed in Wicks Volume 1 (1950), covering the years 1800–1815. Of those 31 plays, 24 were obtained from Google Books, Gallica and other sources. These works have been converted to full text, cleaned and formatted. They are currently available for free download and collaboration on GitHub.

Keywords Digital humanities; Napoleon; Paris; Theater; Corpus design

4.1 A Broader View of the Parisian Stage in the Early Nineteenth Century

In Chap. 3, we saw that FRANTEXT's sources for the literary histories of the nineteenth century were narrowly focused on upper-class tastes. Since the compilation of FRANTEXT, several histories have examined theaters that cater to the rest of the population, including Carlson (1972), Degaine (1992) and McCormick (1993). The catalog of premières compiled by Wicks (1950 et seq.), which forms the basis for this book, may have influenced these writers. In this section I will synthesize these histories into a short history of French popular theater in the early nineteenth century.

© The Author(s) 2019
A. Grieve-Smith, *Building a Representative Theater Corpus*,
https://doi.org/10.1007/978-3-030-32402-5_4

For 400 years during the Middle Ages, the kings of France had granted a monopoly on theatrical performances to the Confrères de la Passion. After a turbulent period in the sixteenth century, the Comédie-Française obtained the monopoly on spoken theater. In 1791 the National Assembly ended that monopoly, and within the next few years over 30 new theaters had opened. The center of this theater district was the Boulevard du Temple at the edge of the Marais, nicknamed the Boulevard du Crime because theaters on that boulevard showed many melodramas involving criminal acts.

The boom in theaters brought on a wave of creativity, including many plays catering to lower and middle classes, with greater representation on stage for members of those classes. In just 16 years, 1800 through 1815, a total of 3017 plays premièred in Paris. Wicks (1950) lists 749 of these as comedies, 346 as vaudevilles and 276 as melodramas; there are only 50 dramas and 32 tragedies in the catalog.

As with many of the new freedoms in the French Revolution, liberty on the stage was gradually reined in over the next few decades. On August 2, 1793, the National Convention reimposed censorship. In 1799 Napoleon granted subsidies to the Théâtre Français, successor to the Comédie-Française, and then set about reorganizing the other theaters, closing some and establishing subsidies for others. In a series of decrees in 1807 he divided the Parisian scene into four *grands théâtres* (the Théâtre Français, later renamed the Empereur; the Opéra-Comique; the Opéra; and the Louvois, renamed the Théâtre de l'Impératrice) and four *théâtres secondaires* (the Gaîté, the Ambigu-Comique, the Variétés and the Vaudeville). The Théâtre de la Porte-Saint-Martin had been designated as a secondary theater in the decree of April 25, but was closed in the decree of July 29 (Table 4.1).

The theaters had already tended to specialize, and the decrees of 1807 prescribed specific repertoires for each theater. "None of the theaters of Paris will be allowed to perform plays outside of the genre that is assigned to them" (April 25 decree, Article 5).

A handful of other venues were licensed to provide other entertainment, such as the Cirque Olympique for equestrian demonstrations and the Acrobates and Funambules for rope-dancing. All of them pushed the limits of their licenses toward theatrical productions, with mute pantomimes and occasionally spoken ones. Theaters were also licensed in suburbs like Belleville, Montmartre and Montparnasse, all of which are now within Paris proper.

Table 4.1 Theaters designated as *grands théâtres* or *théâtres secondaires*, and their designated genres, under the Napoleonic decrees of 1807

Wicks abbreviation	Rank	Name	Alternate name(s)	Genres
TF	Grand	Théâtre Français	Comédie-Française, Théâtre de l'Empereur	Tragedy, comedy
LOD	Grand	Théâtre de l'Impératrice	Théâtre de la rue Louvois, Comédie de l'Odéon	Tragedy, comedy
AIM	Grand	Opéra	Académie Impériale de Musique	Opera, ballet
OC	Grand	Opéra-Comique		Musical theater
	Grand	Opera-Buffa		Plays in Italian
TV	Secondary	Théâtre du Vaudeville		Vaudeville
TMV, TVR	Secondary	Théâtre des Variétés	Théâtre Montansier-Variétés	Grivois, poissard, villageois
PSM	Secondary/ closed	Théâtre de la Porte saint-Martin		Melodrama
TG, TC	Secondary	Théâtre de la Gaîté	Théâtre de la Cité	Pantomimes, harlequinades, farces
TAC	Secondary	Théâtre de l'Ambigu-Comique		Melodrama, pantomimes, harlequinades, farces
	Secondary	Théâtre des Variétés Etrangères		Plays in other languages
JG	Tolerated	Jeux Gymniques		
TJA	Closed	Théâtre des Jeunes Artistes		
TNT	Closed	Théâtre des Nouveaux Troubadours	Théâtre des Variétés Amusantes	

Napoleon also established theaters in his country house at the Malmaison and the imperial palace at Saint-Cloud, where he and the court viewed command performances, mostly by the company of the Théâtre de l'Empereur. He also summoned that troupe to follow him on campaign, with performances in Brussels in 1804, Erfurt in 1808 and Dresden in 1813. He micromanaged productions, writing letters from Moscow to attempt to resolve disputes among actors.

After Napoleon's defeat the restored Louis XVIII kept the basic structure of eight theaters, but his control and censorship were much lighter than that under the Empire. Censorship would be lifted several times during the rest of the century, after each revolution: 1830, 1848 and 1871. Each time it would be reimposed after a few years, with the longest period without censorship lasting from 1830 through 1835.

4.2   Charles Beaumont Wicks and *The Parisian Stage*

The Digital Parisian Stage project aims to be the first representative historical corpus of French. In order to improve on FRANTEXT we need a more representative sample. For that, we will need a good sampling frame. We need first a category of texts that relates to our research question, and second an exhaustive list of texts in that category that we can use as the basis for our sample.

Thanks to a lifetime of work by Charles Beaumont Wicks, we have such a list for nineteenth-century theaters. Wicks's five-volume work, The Parisian Stage, is a list of every play that premièred in Paris in the nineteenth century, compiled from listings and reviews in contemporary newspapers and secondary sources (Wicks 1950: vii).

The first volume (Wicks 1950) lists 3017 plays from the years 1800 through 1815, roughly corresponding to Napoleon's time as First Consul and then Emperor of France. The second lists 3080 plays from 1816 through 1830, corresponding to the Restoration reigns of Louis XVIII and Charles X. The third, 8013 plays from 1831 through 1850, approximately covers the July Monarchy of Louis-Philippe, and the fourth, 8425 plays from 1851–1875, covers the Second Republic and the Second Empire of Napoleon III. The fifth volume lists 9339 Third Republic plays, from 1875 through the end of the century.

4.3   Scientific Corpora in the Twenty-First Century

In the twenty-first century the technological landscape is very different from the one faced by the compilers of the *Trésor de la langue française*. The expense of compiling a corpus no longer needs to be justified by a dictionary, largely because nothing needs to be printed. The smartphone that I am currently writing this paragraph on has more computing power than a Bull Gamma 60. The World Wide Web is available to virtually the entire population of Europe and North America, and a large percentage of the rest of the world. Hosting a text database and a concordance application is within the budget of every university, and that of many individuals. Copies can even be hosted for free on sites like GitHub, as I will describe later in this chapter.

More recent advances have made the compilation of corpora much easier. Massive scanning projects like Google Books and Gallica (the online repository of the National Library of France) have brought the collections of many research libraries online. Advances in consumer-grade optical character recognition have made it easier to convert scanned texts to computer-readable, easily annotatable forms. Building on these resources and technological advances, a small group or even an individual can compile a new corpus and put it online in a fraction of the time it took the CNRS to create FRANTEXT. There is no need to cater to the "cultivated man," no need to sell copies at all. It can all be done by students, by researchers or by hobbyists.

One particularly intriguing aspect of twenty-first-century publishing is that the World Wide Web and public collaborative sites like GitHub and Google Docs enable short publication times and real-time collaboration. One result of this is that people from around the world can collaborate easily on compiling and refining a corpus. Another is that a corpus can be made available in increments, as texts reach a certain level of quality. New texts can be added, and existing texts corrected and released as they are ready. For example, Volumes 2–5 of *The Parisian Stage* (Wicks 1952 et seq.) contain errata sections listing revisions, additions and deletions to previous volumes. A present-day version of the catalog hosted on GitHub improves greatly on this process, simply allowing users to download the latest version, or to "pull a diff" containing changes from a preceding version.

This facilitates the development of a more broadly representative corpus, one more in line with the original intent of the creators of FRANTEXT. A more representative corpus would give us more reliable answers to questions about how language varies and changes. I intend the Digital Parisian Stage corpus to be the start of just such a corpus.

4.4   Sampling *The Parisian Stage*

I converted the first volume of *The Parisian Stage* (Wicks 1950) into an electronic database and then sampled 31 plays at random, 1% of the total; see Appendix A for the list. For this study I have weighted all plays equally, but this is a decision that has implications for representativeness. A further study could take into account the number of times that each play was staged, the number of tickets sold and other indicators of influence to the extent such information is available.

Most of the playwrights in the corpus only authored one play in the sample, but there were four (Bawr, Brazier, Chazet and Sewrin) who contributed to two plays each, as follows:

- Sophie de Bawr wrote both *Le Rival obligeant* (1803) and *La Méprise* (1815). The script of *La Méprise* was never published, and as of publication of the current volume I have been unable to obtain a manuscript.
- Nicolas Brazier contributed to both *La Chaumière au pied des Alpes* (1810) and *Les Petits braconniers* (1813). These two plays have very different levels of *ne* alone and left dislocation, which suggests that Brazier did not impose a consistent style on both plays.
- René de Chazet contributed to both *Les Acteurs à l'épreuve* (1808) and *Avis aux jaloux* (1809). These also have very different levels of those two variables.
- Sewrin wrote *Jocrisse-Maître et Jocrisse-Valet* (1810) and collaborated with Chazet on *Les Acteurs à l'épreuve*. These have similar levels of the two variables, especially low left dislocation, but this could be due to the similarity in the two genres (comedy and vaudeville, respectively).

4.5   Compiling and Distributing a Full-Text Corpus

There are 31 listings in the sample, but three of these are likely errors:

- *Plus de peur que de mal* (Théâtre du Marais, 1803/an XI). A listing in Kennedy et al. (1996: 189) suggests that this was a performance of a play by Radet, Desfontaines and Fouques that premièred in 1793, also known as *La Gageure Inutile*.
- *Le Compère futaille* (Théâtre des Étrangers, 1803). Wicks (1961: 223) lists this as being performed at the Théâtre du Marais, but both the *Journal de Paris* and the *Journal des Débats et Décrets* list it as being performed at the Théâtre des Étrangers "(Ci-devant du

Marais.).'" Wicks generally did not include the Théâtre des Étrangers in his catalog because it featured mostly plays in translation.

- *Les Trois damis*, premièred at the Théâtre de la Société Olympique in 1804. Lecomte (1908: 115) credits this to Bodard de Tézay, but Bodard's play was performed and published in 1785, making this a revival. Wicks typically did not include revivals in his catalog, only original premières, and in this sample I follow his lead.

Six other plays met with little enough success that they were never published:

- *L'Abbaye de Graswille* (mélo., Théâtre du Marais, 1804). I have found no evidence that a play of this exact name was ever performed. A play called *L'Abbaye de Grasville*, by Jean-Bernard-Eugène Cantiran de Boirie and Jean-Marie-Bernard Clément, is listed with no date or venue of performance in the Instructions Générales of Sauvan (1806: 3), and in Louandre and Bourquelot's biographical sketch of Boirie (1846: vol. 2, page 95). This play is also listed in the catalog of the Société des auteurs et compositeurs dramatiques (SACD, 1863), but is not available online.
- *Le Baron de Felsheim* (mélo.-com., Mme de Beaunoir, Théâtre de la Porte Saint-Martin, 1805). According to the *Opinion du parterre* (Valleran 1806: 369), this closed after only three performances. Mme de Beaunoir was the pseudonym of Alexandre-Louis-Bertrand Robineau, who wrote some 200 plays, of which only 30 were ever published (Abbott 1936).
- *La Dame invisible* (vaud., Armand-François Chateauvieux, Armand Croizette and Etienne-Claude Fleureau de Ligny, Théâtre Montansier-Variétés, 1800). There are several plays with this title and subtitle from different eras, but multiple contemporary newspapers list this as an original work. A review in the *Courrier des spectacles* (19 germinal) reported that it had achieved almost no success. This play is listed in the SACD catalog (1863), but is not available online.
- *L'Epreuve excusable* (com., Prosper Leroi de Neufvillette, Théâtre de la Gaîté, 1808). According to Lecomte (1910: 208), this was never printed.
- *La Méprise* (com., Sophie de Bawr, 1815): This play closed after five performances at the Comédie-Française (Rabbe et al. 1834: 42).

According to letters stored in the Comédie-Française archives, the theater management requested permission to send the play to other theaters, and Bawr granted that permission, but as of publication I have found no evidence of any further performances, and no manuscript.

- *Avis aux jaloux* (op.-com., René Alissan de Chazet and Maurice Ourry, 1815) was only available in manuscript form, from the archives of the Opéra-Comique on dezede.com. I have included it in the available texts.

If we assume that the proportions are similar for the whole of Wicks's catalog, this means that of the 3017 plays listed in Wicks (1950), roughly 300 are errors and 2300 are available online.

The other 22 plays were published and made available in full text, and have been included. One play, *La Chaumière au pied des Alpes* (Théodore Maillard and Jean-Baptiste-Augustin Hapdé, 1810) is available on microfilm as part of ProQuest's OmniSys World Literature Collection. The remaining plays are all available through Google Books, some with additional copies available from the Gallica website of the Bibliothèque Nationale de France, the Internet Archive and the University of Warwick's Marandet collection.

The vast majority of the plays were only available in scanned image form, so I used ABBYY FineReader optical character recognition to convert them to full-text format, and edited the resulting files to remove errors and provide consistent formatting and metadata.

I have made the 1% sample list and the full texts available on the software collaboration repository GitHub. In this choice I was inspired by authorship models that have been used in recent digital humanities literature, for example Tenen and Wythoff (2018). Sharing this corpus free of charge allows scholars to use it for any other purpose, including checking my work and running their preferred corpus analysis tools on the data. Publishing it on a collaborative platform like GitHub allows others to correct errors in the underlying texts, and to expand the corpus to include other texts.

4.6   FORMATTING AND SEPARATING TEXT

I chose to format the texts in HTML 5, keeping the markup simple, with the following tags:

- <div class="Content" />: Each play has one Content tag containing all the content of the play, separate from any front matter or HTML headers or footers.
- <h1 class="act" />: An act in the play.
- <h2 class="scene" />: A scene in the play.
- <p class="stage" />: Stage directions, including lists of characters in a scene and identification of melodies used in songs.
- <p class="charn$x$" />: Identification of which character's lines come next. The characters are identified by a number (located where x is here) indicating the order of appearance.
- <p class="char$x$" />: Lines spoken by character number x.
- <p class="pagenum" />: A page number as marked in the printed or manuscript text.
- <p class="heading" />: A running heading at the top of a printed or manuscript page.

I marked the lines to identify which character speaks them, because there is wide variation among characters, even within a single play. The plots of many plays turn on the social categories that characters belong to—economic classes, genders, regional origins, migrant populations. These categories are frequently heard—and read—in features of the characters' language. As we will see in the case studies, marking these categories allows us to document this language variation. This in turn helps us to understand how the Principle of Authority biases the FRANTEXT corpus.

Most of the plays included a table of characters at the beginning. I formatted all such tables as simple HTML tables, with no additional markup. Some plays used braces to indicate simultaneous speech or song by multiple characters. In these cases I attempted to mark the simultaneity as clearly as possible.

REFERENCES

Abbott, Elizabeth-Béatrice. 1936. Robineau, dit de Beaunoir, et les petits théâtres du XVIIIe Siècle. *Revue d'Histoire littéraire de la France* 43: 2.

Carlson, Marvin. 1972. *The French Stage in the Nineteenth Century*. Metuchen: Scarecrow.

Degaine, André. 1992. *Histoire du théâtre dessinée: de la préhistoire à nos jours, tous les temps et tous les pays*. Paris: Nizet.

Kennedy, Emmet, Marie-Laurence Netter, James P. McGregor, and Mark V. Olsen. 1996. *Theatre, Opera, and Audiences in Revolutionary Paris: Analysis and Repertory*. Westport: Greenwood.

Lecomte, Louis-Henry. 1908. *Les Variétés Amusantes. Histoire des théâtres de Paris*. Paris: Daragon.

———. 1910. *Les Variétés Amusantes. Histoire des théâtres de Paris*. Paris: Daragon.

Louandre, Charles, and Félix Bourquelot. 1846. *La littérature française contemporaine 1827–1844, Volume 2*. Paris: Daguin.

McCormick, John. 1993. *Popular Theatres of Nineteenth Century France*. London: Routledge.

Rabbe, Alphonse, Claude Vieilh de Boisjoslin, and François Georges Binet de Sainte-Preuve. 1834. *Biographie universelle et portative des contemporains*. Paris: Levrault.

Sauvan. 1806. *Instructions générales, suivies des lois relatives à la propriété dramatique, & de la liste générale des auteurs signataires de la procuration de M. Sauvan*. Paris: Sauvan.

Société des auteurs et compositeurs dramatiques. 1863. *Catalogue général des oeuvres dramatiques et lyriques faisant partie du répertoire*. Paris: Guyot.

Tenen, Denis, and Grant Wythoff. 2018. Sustainable Authorship in Plain Text using Pandoc and Markdown. *The Programming Historian*. https://programminghistorian.org/en/lessons/sustainable-authorship-in-plain-text-using-pandoc-and-markdown.

Valleran. 1806. *L'opinion du Parterre, ou revue des théâtres*. Paris: Martinet.

Wicks, Charles Beaumont. 1950, 1952, 1961, 1967, 1979. *The Parisian Stage*. Tuscaloosa: University of Alabama.

CHAPTER 5

Case Study 1: The Spread of Change in French Negation

Abstract French is an example of Jespersen's Cycle (*Negation in English and Other Languages*. Copenhagen: Munksgaard, 1917), with a shift from *ne* alone to *ne ... pas* to *pas* alone over the past 500 years. Grieve-Smith (*The Spread of Change in French Negation*. Ph.D. diss., University of New Mexico, 2009) found that in Old French *ne ... pas* appears predominantly in contexts that are consistent with presupposition denial but increased in frequency from the sixteenth through twentieth centuries, appearing in predicate negation contexts. This fits with Kroch's (*Language Variation and Change* 1: 199–244, 1989) application of Verhulst's (*Correspondence Mathématiques et Physiques* 10: 113, 1838) logistic model of population increase, which can be explained by Bybee's (*Language and Cognitive Processes* 10 (425)–455, 1995) connection of type frequency to analogical extension. Unfortunately, the concerns about representativeness raised in Chap. 2 apply to this study. Texts in the Digital Parisian Stage corpus have a significantly lower token frequency of *ne* alone than those in FRANTEXT for 1800–1815.

Keywords Jespersen's Cycle; Negation; French; Corpus; Syntax

In Chap. 3 I described the "Principle of Authority" used to compile the FRANTEXT corpus, and in Chap. 4 I discussed a new corpus, the Digital Parisian Stage, based on a representative sample. We would expect these

© The Author(s) 2019
A. Grieve-Smith, *Building a Representative Theater Corpus*,
https://doi.org/10.1007/978-3-030-32402-5_5

two corpora to differ in measurable ways because the application of a Principle of Authority would result in a corpus of texts that were representative of the artistic and class interests of the authorities consulted, while a random sample would result in texts representative of what was performed in theaters, or at least of what has been preserved. As a test of this hypothesis I annotated the plays available from the Digital Parisian Stage corpus for sentence negation and compared the results with those from the four FRANTEXT plays for the same period (1800–1815).

5.1   DECLARATIVE SENTENCE NEGATION IN FRENCH

The form of declarative sentence negation is a longstanding object of interest in French linguistics, notably as a featured example of Jespersen's Cycle (Jespersen 1917). My doctoral dissertation (Grieve-Smith 2009) was based on an investigation of declarative sentence negation in FRANTEXT theatrical texts, supplemented with additional theatrical texts from earlier periods. My dissertation study and this book are complementary: I created the Digital Parisian Stage corpus because I was dissatisfied with FRANTEXT in my study of declarative sentence negation, and now in this book I have used declarative sentence negation to test the Digital Parisian Stage corpus.

In the nineteenth century there were three main ways to negate a sentence in French: *ne* alone (typically before the verb), *ne* before and *pas* after, and *ne ... point*, as shown in the following examples from the Digital Parisian Stage corpus:

1. CHARLES: *et je suis peut-être le seul qui **ne** puisse avoir un billet pour la représentation de ma pièce.* (la Jeunesse de Favart, 1809)
   CHARLES: and I am perhaps the only one who cannot get a ticket for the performance of my own play.
2. ANSELME: *C'est être bien hardi, après toutes les menaces que vous avez osé me faire si je **ne** vous donnais **pas** ma fille ....* (le Grenadier de Louis XV, 1815)
   ANSELME: This is very brazen of you, after all the threats that you have dared make to me if I did not give you my daughter.
3. ROSERDORF: *Malheureux, vous m'avez consolé, pauvre, vous m'avez secouru, blessé, vous **n'avez point** dédaigné de me penser vous-même ....* (Les Strélitz, 1808)
   ROSERDORF: I was unhappy and you consoled me; I was poor and you helped me; I was wounded and you did not disdain to think of me yourself ....

In Old French these three constructions coexisted with another negator, *ne ... mie*. In each of the "embracing" constructions the postverbal element is related to a nominal: *pas* "step, pace," *point* "point (in time)" and *mie* "crumb." This suggests that these constructions evolved out of phrases using those words, and indeed Diez (1882) finds *ne punctum quidam (temporis)* used by Cicero, and *non micam panis* used by Petronius. Some authors (e.g., Lüdtke 1979: 246) have gone further to assert, with no evidence, that similar phrases were used for *pas* in Vulgar Latin or Old French. Schweighäuser (1852) undertakes a detailed investigation of the use of these constructions in Latin and Old French, concluding, "Let us note in any case that this modification undergone by the sense of the word *pas* took place prior to the most ancient relics of the language."

The differences among the three embracing negation constructions in Old French were minimal. Price (1997) gives an overview of some of the claimed differences. The strongest difference he finds is that, at least before the seventeenth century, *ne ... point* tended to be used more with the partitive construction, a characteristic feature of French used to express quantity. Price also found significant regional variation in the use of these negative constructions. While *ne ... pas* predominated in Paris, Normandy and England, *ne ... mie* was more common in Northern and Eastern France, particularly Lorraine and Picardy.

In spite of these geographical and usage differences, Price observed that many authors used several sentence negators almost interchangeably in a single text, regardless of their dialect background. He gives two possible motivations for this. One is for rhyme: since all four negators ended in different sounds, it was easy to substitute one for another to make a better rhyme. Another is to avoid repetition: an author could vary the sound of a text by using different negators. Offord (1976: 332) observes that "MS [manuscript] variants testify to the interchangeability of the particles," tallying 12 examples in the *Roman de Berinus* where one manuscript might have *ne ... mie* but another might have *ne ... pas*. He does not mention any similar variation for *ne* alone versus one of the embracing negation constructions.

5.2   Emphatic Negation and Presupposition Denial in English, Catalan and Italian

Even if the differences between the three embracing negators were difficult to tease apart, in the Spread of Change corpus I found clear differences between the embracing negators and *ne* alone before 1500. At the suggestion of Scott Schwenter, I used Geurts's (1998) framework to capture these differences, particularly the distinction between predicate negation, proposition denial and presupposition denial, as illustrated by the following examples:

4. Kurt **doesn't** realize that his camels have been kidnapped.
   Geurts 1998, example 1a
5. A: The cook is guilty.
   B: The cook is **not** guilty.
   Geurts 1998, example 4
6. Kurt DOESN'T realize that his camels have been kidnapped, because they **HAVEN'T** been kidnapped.
   Geurts 1998, example 1b

The first sentence is predicate negation, a simple statement of fact that happens to be negative: Kurt happens not to realize a particular state of affairs. The second is proposition denial: speaker A asserts the proposition that the cook is guilty, and speaker B denies that proposition. The "HAVEN'T" in the third sentence, written in all caps by Geurts to indicate contrastive stress in English, is an example of presupposition denial: it identifies the presupposition that the camels have been kidnapped and denies it.

In his 2006 paper, "Fine-Tuning Jespersen's Cycle," Schwenter identifies similar distinctions in Catalan and Italian and building on Israel (1998), argues that they correspond to Jespersen's (1917) distinction between normal and "emphatic" negations, as in the following examples:

7. [Stepping outside on a fairly warm day, after several days of unusually cold weather]
   Avui no fa fred.
   "Today it's not cold."
   Schwenter, Catalan example 2b
8. [Same weather scenario as in (2a)]
   A: *Avui fa fred també?*
   "Will be it cold today as well?"
   B: *No, avui no fa pas fred.*
   "No, today it's not cold."
   Schwenter, Catalan example 3a
9. [speaker B sees interlocutor A putting on a heavy coat]
   Avui no fa pas fred.
   "Today it's not cold."
   Schwenter, Catalan example 3b

In the first of these examples, preverbal no by itself is used to indicate predicate negation, while in the second example *no ... pas* (cognate with French *ne ... pas*) is used to indicate proposition denial. In the third example, speaker B is using *no ... pas* to indicate denial of speaker A's presupposition that it is cold, indicated by the nonverbal act of putting on a heavy coat. Schwenter (2006: 6) argues that both uses of *no ... pas* fall within Jespersen's (and Israel's) category of "emphatic" negation.

Schwenter then applies this analysis to Italian examples given by Zanuttini (1997):

10. A: *Chi viene a prenderti?*
    "Who's coming to pick you up?"
    B: *Non so. Ma Gianni **non** ha la macchina.*
    "I don't know. But Gianni doesn't have the car."
    Schwenter, Italian example 6a, from Zanuttini 1997
11. A: *Chi viene a prenderti, Gianni?*
    "Who's coming to pick you up, Gianni?"
    B: *Non so. Ma Gianni **non** ha **mica** la macchina.*
    "I don't know. But Gianni doesn't have the car."
    Schwenter, Italian example 6b, from Zanuttini 1997

In the first example, there is no overt presupposition that Gianni might have the car, so that predicate is negated with a simple preverbal *non*. In the second, speaker A's overt acknowledgment of the possibility that Gianni might be coming to pick up speaker B indicates a presupposition that Gianni has the car, which can then be denied using *non ... mica* (cognate with French *ne ... mie*).

5.3   Emphatic Negation and Presupposition Denial in Old French

Schwenter (2006) argues that his examples from Catalan and Zanuttini's examples from Italian help explain the constructed Old French examples he cites from multiple sources, such as Schwegler (1988). But does this work beyond constructed examples for actual corpus data? For my dissertation, *the Spread of Change in French Negation* (Grieve-Smith 2009: 104–109) I assembled a corpus extending from the earliest theatrical text in Old French through the twentieth century, which I will call the Spread of Change corpus.

FRANTEXT has been extended to include texts from the seventeenth and eighteenth centuries as well as nineteenth and twentieth centuries, so I took a sample for that period of one play from every quarter century. FRANTEXT still had almost nothing from before 1600 and a limited selection from the early seventeenth century; I compiled a corpus from what was available. Issues of bias and representativeness were similar to those I identified for nineteenth-century French theater in Chap. 3; the biggest difference is that the number of texts that were written down and preserved before movable type and widespread literacy is much smaller than those from the nineteenth century; accordingly, I annotated every play I could find from before 1548.

I was not able to restrict the Spread of Change corpus to Parisian French. We have only one play from the twelfth century, the Anglo-Norman *Ordo Representacionis Ade*, thought to have been written around 1160. The historical record contains very few plays from Paris in the thirteenth century; I supplemented the corpus with Picard plays, but these may be very different from Parisian plays. The vast majority of texts from the fourteenth century come from one series of miracle plays performed by the Parisian goldsmiths' guild; presumably there were many other plays performed during that century, but these are the only ones in the corpus. The biases that exist in this corpus are thus inherited from the biases of medieval publication and preservation.

In the Spread of Change corpus I found confirmation of Schwenter's (2006) hypothesis that the Old French negation constructions *ne* alone, *ne ... pas*, *ne ... point* and *ne ... mie* followed a similar pattern to present-day Catalan and Italian. I categorized each negation in the corpus as predicate negation, proposition denial or presupposition denial, based on whether there was an overt or implicit statement of the denied proposition in the preceding discourse.

One challenge was that I found a large number of negations where the existence of a denied presupposition could not be conclusively determined. Rather than an insurmountable obstacle, this result actually confirmed Traugott's (1989) observation that semantic change proceeds through polysemy and ambiguity. I chose to count those ambiguous instances separately, alongside unambiguous instances of presupposition denial and predicate negation. The results are in Tables 5.1, 5.2 and 5.3:

For the period 1100–1600, *ne* alone is used in more than 90% of instances of unambiguous predicate negation, and in more than 75% of declarative sentence negations that were ambiguous between predicate

Table 5.1 Syntactic realizations of negation in unambiguous predicate negation contexts

Century	ne *alone (%)*	ne ... pas *(%)*	ne ... point *(%)*	ne ... mie *(%)*
12th	100.0	0.0	0.0	0.0
13th	100.0	0.0	0.0	0.0
14th	98.4	0.8	0.8	0.0
15th	100.0	0.0	0.0	0.0
16th	98.4	0.5	1.2	0.0
17th	86.2	6.9	6.9	0.0
18th	69.5	25.4	5.1	0.0
19th	23.3	74.8	1.9	0.0
20th	7.1	85.7	7.1	0.0

Table 5.2 Syntactic realizations of negation in contexts ambiguous between predicate negation and presupposition denial

Century	ne *alone (%)*	ne ... pas *(%)*	ne ... point *(%)*	ne ... mie *(%)*
12th	87.5	12.5	0.0	0.0
13th	74.4	10.2	2.3	13.1
14th	81.0	12.0	3.2	3.8
15th	80.9	12.3	5.6	1.2
16th	81.3	7.2	11.1	0.3
17th	41.6	30.7	27.7	0.0
18th	27.0	50.3	22.7	0.0
19th	15.3	80.1	4.5	0.0
20th	8.4	90.0	1.6	0.0

Table 5.3 Syntactic realizations of negation in unambiguous presupposition denial contexts

Century	ne *alone (%)*	ne ... pas *(%)*	ne ... point *(%)*	ne ... mie *(%)*
12th	16.7	83.3	0.0	0.0
13th	27.4	21.1	10.5	41.1
14th	11.7	48.6	19.8	19.8
15th	19.6	45.1	31.9	3.4
16th	27.1	41.9	27.8	3.3
17th	9.7	45.6	44.7	0.0
18th	1.4	61.5	37.1	0.0
19th	1.5	93.8	4.6	0.0
20th	1.5	96.0	2.5	0.0

negation and presupposition denial. It was occasionally used in contexts with unambiguous presupposition denial, but less than 15% of the time, except for the thirteenth century when it is used 23% of the time; this may be due to the preponderance of Picard data. The two-part negations, *ne ... pas*, *ne ... point* and *ne ... mie*, were used the rest of the time, in proportions that fit the observations of Price (1997) and Offord (1976) that I described above.

The use of *ne ... mie* is quite rare after 1600, especially in Parisian theater, so it does not appear in my corpus after that. From then on, *ne ... pas* was used more and more frequently in contexts that are ambiguous between predicate negation and presupposition denial: 31% in the seventeenth century and 51% in the eighteenth. It also began to be used in unambiguous predicate negation contexts, but with a delay: 7% of instances of unambiguous predicate negation and 26% in the eighteenth.

The use of *ne ... point* is similar to that of *ne ... pas* in the seventeenth century, but then it declines. It is used in 28% of contexts that are ambiguous between predicate negation and presupposition denial in the seventeenth century, but only 19% in the eighteenth. Similarly, it is used in 4% of unambiguous predicate negation in the seventeenth and eighteenth centuries.

These results suggest that in Old French there were clear distinctions of meaning and use among the three constructions, but those distinctions seem to have collapsed some time during the sixteenth century. Since then, playwrights have used *ne ... pas* in an increasing number of contexts where previous generations used *ne* alone or *ne ... point*, suggesting a similar change in the language as a whole.

5.4   ANALOGICAL EXTENSION OF *NE ... PAS*

The reanalysis of *ne ... pas* as an expression of unemphatic predicate negation meant that from the seventeenth century on there were two constructions to express predicate negation, preverbal *ne* alone and *ne ... pas*, with no clear semantic distinction between them. As I mentioned in Chap. 2, Croft's First Law of Propagation (2000: 176) states that one way language users eliminate this kind of overlap is to shift to one variant or another. The data in the Spread of Change corpus show that this is what occurred with predicate negation in French.

After a reanalysis like this, typically there remains a legacy pattern that reflects the earlier usage. When *ne ... pas* was used for presupposition

Table 5.4 Negation in declarative sentences by century

Century	ne *alone*	ne ... pas	ne ... point	ne ... mie	*Total*
12th	48	13			61
13th	253	39	14	63	369
14th	268	75	29	28	400
15th	308	112	75	10	505
16th	825	195	159	14	1193
17th	285	210	200		695
18th	128	396	207		731
19th	113	921	37		1071
20th	25	446	10		481
Total	2253	2407	731	115	5506

denial before 1600, it primarily appeared in focused positions like main clauses and with verbs like *aimer*, *dire* and *falloir* whose presuppositions might be denied. Preverbal *ne* alone appeared more frequently in subordinate clauses, with expressions of causation, and with verbs like *savoir*, *pouvoir* and *oser*, whose negations tend to be reported as simple matters of fact.

This pattern persisted after the reanalysis, as described by Maupas (1607), Vaugelas (1647) and Ewert (1943), but gradually began to change, as I found in my Spread of Change corpus. Table 5.4 shows the number of tokens used in each construction per century:

Figure 5.1 shows this data as a stacked area chart.

The rise of *ne ... pas*, and the rise of two-part negation in general, follows a pattern that has been observed many times in language change over the past 70 years. This S-curve was first noted by Osgood and Sebeok (1954: 155), but they did not explore it beyond the simple statement that the data resembled an S. Altmann et al. (1983: 111) proposed a logistic function to model observations detailing the acceptance of Arabic loanwords in Persian prose and draw parallels with other phenomena: "The same dependence is observed in other fields of science as in the theory of growth, in epidemics, etc. [...] We consider this analogy to be a strong argument for the validity of the model." Kroch (1982, 1989) put forth the logistic function for similar reasons: "its use is generally considered appropriate in statistical studies of changing percentages of alternating forms over time" (Kroch 1989: 4).

The logistic model was created by Verhulst (1838) to model the exact same pattern observed in population changes by Malthus (1789). In these cases, a population increases in size as time goes on: slowly at first and then

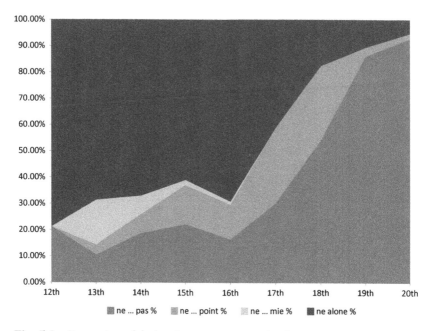

Fig. 5.1 Expression of declarative sentence negation by century

quickly. As the population approaches the carrying capacity of the land, there are checks on that growth, and the increase slows. Verhulst noted "the speed of growth is slowed by the very increase in the number of inhabitants."

The logistic model has been applied to autocatalytic reactions in chemistry and technology adoption in history. It is likely to fit any circumstance where the growth in number is dependent on the number itself and limited by the total capacity. In language it applies to situations governed by Croft's First Law of Propagation (2000: 176) because in this propagation the growth in the usage of a construction is proportional to its usage and limited by the total potential usage. In usage-based theory of propagation, these forces are known as analogical extension and entrenchment, respectively.

Analogical extension is a well-documented (Meillet 1912; Hock 2003) process whereby a construction that has high type frequency tends to be used with even more types. The notion of type frequency is a difficult one in usage-based linguistics, and merits some elaboration. The most important point is that it is always used in the context of Croft's First Law of

Propagation: it is a way of understanding the relationship between multiple ways of fulfilling the same linguistic function. In this case, we are interested in multiple ways of expressing predicate negation: *ne* alone versus *ne ... pas* and *ne ... point*.

In a corpus we find many tokens of predicate negation: individual instances, each with their specific circumstances. According to the usage-based theory of propagation, language users form schemas across these instances, which we refer to as types (Zager 1981; Bybee 1995). When investigating a change, we can create a hypothetical set of types that may reflect the types the language users have formed. In the case of predicate negation on the Parisian stage, I hypothesized that the playwrights were forming types based on verbs that occurred in these tokens of negation. There are a finite number of types in each user's memory, and these types constitute the envelope of variation (Labov 1972) of the change.

Analogical extension occurs, according to the usage-based theory, when language users want to produce a type, but forget which construction is used with that type in the legacy pattern (Goldberg 2006). They will then make a guess and assign the type to a construction at random, with the probability of each construction weighted by its existing type frequency. The result is that the constructions with higher type frequency tend to acquire even more types, which is exactly the kind of driving force behind Verhulst's logistic model.

Analogical extension also happens when a language user learns a new type and needs to decide which construction to use that type with, but the number of new types added to a language in one user's lifetime tends to be relatively small. Because of this, the total number of types—the envelope of variation—tends to stay relatively stable, and most of the increase of one construction comes from forgetting the old patterns of usage that went with other constructions.

The forgetting that is necessary for a type to move from one construction to another does not happen evenly across the lexicon. Some types are more entrenched in memory (Bybee and Thompson 1997), and thus more likely to continue with the same construction for generations, if not centuries. As Joan Bybee (Hooper 1976) has shown, the entrenchment of a type with a construction is a function of its raw token frequency. Propagation tends to start with the types with lower token frequencies and proceed to higher ones—but the highest ones may continue as relic forms. This corresponds to the checks on increase in populations in the Malthus/Verhulst model.

5.5   COMPETITION FOR USAGE IN PREDICATE NEGATION

The model developed by Verhulst (1838) was based on populations increasing to fill new capacity, either in new lands or with new technologies allowing the existing lands to support more people. This is different from the situation we find in analogical extension, where types shift from one construction to another. A closer analogy would be two populations in competition with each other for the same limited resources.

There is an extension of the Verhulst model for competition, developed independently by Lotka (1925) and Volterra (1926). The case they had in mind was the competition between two species competing for finite resources in the same environment, and Gause (1934) found that it accurately modeled the competitions between two species of Paramecium protozoa for a constant food source, "which always resulted in a complete driving out of *P. caudatum* by *P. aurelia*." The Lotka-Volterra equation is based on the same logistic formula, but for every possible pair of species it adds an interaction coefficient, representing the effect that one species in the pair has on the other.

The S-curve given in Fig. 5.1 represents the percentage of tokens for each negation construction, but I found a similar S-curve for the types (verbs). I applied the Lotka-Volterra model to the proportion of verbs, including all conjugations of the verbs as separate types. I used the least squares method to determine the optimal interaction coefficients, resulting in coefficients predicting a strong effect of *ne … pas* on the other negators, and a relatively weak effect of *ne* alone on *ne … pas*.

Figure 5.2 shows the observed type frequency of *ne* alone for each century, along with the change in type frequency from the previous century, and the change predicted by the Lotka-Volterra model based on the type frequency in the preceding century. Before 1600 the model does not accurately predict the changes in type frequency, but after 1600 it is highly accurate at predicting the type frequency changes of all three negators, with a correlation (Pearson product moment) of 0.93.

5.6   ENTRENCHMENT OF HIGH-FREQUENCY NEGATED FORMS

As I discussed above, Bybee (Hooper 1976; Bybee and Thompson 1997) and others have observed that when there is competition among constructions for the same grammatical function, certain forms get entrenched in

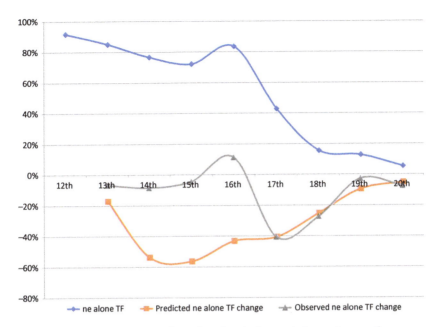

Fig. 5.2 Type frequency, and predicted and observed change in type frequency of preverbal *ne* alone for conjugated verbs, including high-frequency verbs and hapaxes

memory with certain constructions. What I found in the dissertation study was that the entrenchment of forms with preverbal *ne* alone observed by Maupas (1607) and others fit with the pragmatics of predicate negation. This includes not just verbs like *savoir* (example 12), *pouvoir* (example 13), *oser* (example 14) and *venir* but the negation of conditional clauses subordinated with *si* (example 15), complements of another negative (example 16), and complements of expressions of caution (example 17), prevention and causation.

12. FLORVEL: *Je **ne saurais** entrer ici dans le détail....* (Les Mœurs du jour, 1800)
    FLORVEL: I wouldn't be able to get into details here ....
13. ROSERDORF: *Moscou m'est trop connu, je **ne pouvais** m'y tromper.* (Les Strélitz, 1808)
    ROSERDORF: I know Moscow too well, I could not be wrong.

14. SUCHANIN: *il n'osa tremper ses mains dans le sang des Strélitz ....* (Les Strélitz, 1808)
   SUCHANIN: He would not dare to cover his hands in the blood of the Streltsy ....

15. ESOPE: *Je ne vous parlerais pas en faveur de cette union, si je ne connaissais assez le jeune Clitophon pour savoir qu'il doit rendre votre fille heureuse.* (Esope chez Xantus, 1800)
   ESOPE: I would not speak to you in favor of this union, if I did not know young Clitophon well enough to know that he will make your daughter happy.

16. WALLSTEIN: *Des fautes qu'il commit n'accusons que le sort.*
   Il n'est point de courroux que n'appaise la mort. (Wallstein, 1809)
   WALLSTEIN: For the wrongs he committed let us only blame fate.
   There is no fury that death will not appease.

17. LESBIA: *Pour moi, je crains que ma mère ne revienne, et je retourne auprès d'elle.* (Esope chez Xantus, 1800)
   LESBIA: Actually, I think my mother is not coming back, and I will go to her.

In the Spread of Change corpus, I found that the token frequencies of these constructions used with *ne* alone all decreased over time, and that the ones with the highest token frequencies in the sixteenth century tended to be the ones that remained through to the nineteenth and even twentieth centuries. The main exception was with the two most common verbs in the language, *être* and *avoir*, which were commonly used even as main verbs with *ne* alone in the sixteenth century but had completely shifted over to *ne ... pas* by the seventeenth century, except when used as auxiliaries for other verbs.

5.7   STUDYING NEGATION IN THE DIGITAL PARISIAN STAGE CORPUS

The findings from my dissertation—that the Verhulst and Lotka-Volterra models predict the changes in type frequency so closely—were satisfying, but I knew that they were based on a non-representative sample. Could this be a fluke? The usage-based model may apply to elite playwrights learning from earlier playwrights, but does it apply to a broader group of playwrights?

Because of these concerns, after I finished the dissertation study I began work on what became the Digital Parisian Stage corpus. In its current state, the Digital Parisian Stage covers a very limited time frame, from 1800 through 1815, which is only a small fraction of the time frame of this change. I plan to extend the corpus to the entire nineteenth century, and eventually beyond, which will allow me to examine the entire change.

In the short term, it is possible to use the token frequencies of the negation constructions to test whether the Digital Parisian Stage and FRANTEXT produce similar results. If we assume that the general S-curve I identified in the Spread of Change corpus is even remotely accurate (along with other studies like Martineau and Mougeon 2003), we can say that the type frequency of *ne ... pas* tends to increase over the period from 1600 through 1950. We can then consider texts with a greater type frequency for *ne ... pas* to be more advanced in this change, and texts with a lower type frequency to be more conservative, and extend this evaluation to entire corpora.

For this study I chose to exclude one of the plays from the corpus because it contained minimal dialogue. *La Mort du Capitaine Cook* (1814) is an equestrian pantomime adapted from a wildly successful British production. It is a very interesting play in its own right, as it treats the Hawaiian islanders as intelligent humans with a sophisticated social structure, but the printed script mostly consists of descriptions of mimed actions. This leaves 22 plays in the sample.

5.8   Is FRANTEXT More Conservative than the Digital Parisian Stage Corpus?

In comparing the 22 randomly chosen plays from the Digital Parisian Stage corpus with the four plays chosen by the Principle of Authority for the FRANTEXT corpus, I find a significant ($p < 0.01$) difference in the use of sentence negation. The frequencies per play are in the Appendices, and I give a summary below (Table 5.5):

Table 5.5 Declarative sentence negations with *ne* alone, *ne ... pas* and *ne ... point*, in the FRANTEXT and Digital Parisian Stage corpora

	ne *alone*	ne ... pas	ne ... point	*Total negations*	ne (%)	ne ... pas (%)	ne ... point (%)
FRANTEXT	152	268	111	531	29	50	21
Digital Parisian Stage	234	1182	183	1599	15	74	11

In the FRANTEXT plays, *ne … pas* was used in 50% of sentence negations, *ne … point* in 21% and *ne* alone in 29%, while in the Digital Parisian Stage, *ne … pas* was used 74% of the time, *ne … point* 5% and *ne* alone 10% (Figs. 5.3 and 5.4). The individual differences between the two corpora for each negator were statistically significant, with large effect sizes ($d = 1.1$ in both cases) for *ne* alone and *ne … pas*, and a medium effect size for *ne … point* ($d = 0.58$). I also tested for statistical significance on all three measures together for the Digital Parisian Stage as compared to FRANTEXT using a chi-square goodness of fit test ($p < 0.05$).

5.9   A Note on *ne* Dropping

The next stage in the evolution of French negation is the dropping of the *ne* (example 5 in Jespersen 1917: 8). This stage has been attested as far back as the works of Marguerite de Navarre and Nicolas de Troyes in the early sixteenth century (Brunot 1901). By the late twentieth century it was well advanced, as documented by Ashby (1981, 2001) in variationist studies.

Fig. 5.3 The expression of negation in the FRANTEXT corpus

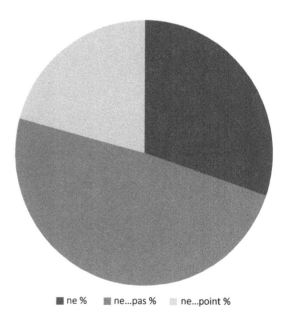

■ ne %   ■ ne…pas %   ▒ ne…point %

Fig. 5.4 The expression of negation in the Digital Parisian Stage corpus

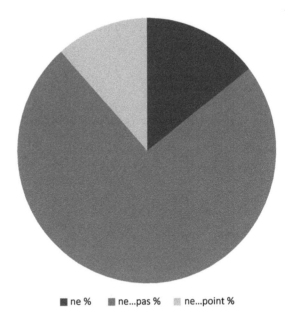

■ ne %   ■ ne...pas %   ▨ ne...point %

Postverbal *pas* alone is not found in any of the FRANTEXT plays from this period, but it does occur in the Digital Parisian Stage sample, including three times in the play *Jocrisse-Maître et Jocrisse-Valet*, by Sewrin, which premièred on October 29, 1810, at the Théâtre des Variétés-Panoramas, as in Example 18.

1. JOCRISSE-VALET: *Vous entendez bien, not' maître, que si j'm appelle jocrisse, c'est pas ma faute; c'est pas moi qui m'a batisé.*
    JOCRISSE-VALET: You understand, m'lord, that just because they call me Jocrisse, it's not my fault. I'm not the one that baptised me.

This is by no means the earliest attestation of *pas* alone in French (see Martineau and Mougeon 2003 for earlier examples), but it indicates that the Digital Parisian Stage corpus includes more representations, if caricatured, of less conservative speech styles than the FRANTEXT plays.

REFERENCES

Altmann, Gabriel, Haro von Buttlar, Walter Rott, and Udo Strauss. 1983. A Law of Change in Language. In *Historical Linguistics*, ed. Barron Brainerd, 104–115. Bochum: Brockmeyer.

Ashby, William J. 1981. The Loss of the Negative Particle *ne* in French: A Syntactic Change in Progress. *Language* 57: 674–687.

———. 2001. Un nouveau regard sur la chute du *ne* en français parlé tourangeau: S'agit-il d'un changement en cours? *JFLS* 11: 1–22.

Brunot, Ferdinand. 1901. *Histoire de la langue française des origines à 1900*. Paris: Armand Colin.

Bybee, Joan. 1995. Regular morphology and the lexicon. *Language and Cognitive Processes* 10: 425–455.

Bybee, Joan, and Sandra A. Thompson. 1997. *Three Frequency Effects in Syntax*. Berkeley: Berkeley Linguistics Society (BLS).

Croft, William. 2000. *Explaining Language Change: An Evolutionary Approach*. London: Longman.

Diez, Friedrich. 1882. *Grammatik der romanischen Sprachen*. Bonn: Eduard Weber's.

Ewert, Alfred. 1943. *The French Language*. London: Faber and Faber.

Gause, Georgyi F. 1934. *The Struggle for Existence*. Baltimore: Williams and Wilkins.

Geurts, Bart. 1998. The Mechanisms of Denial. *Language* 74: 274–307.

Goldberg, Adele E. 2006. *Constructions at Work: The Nature of Generalization in Language*. Oxford: Oxford University Press.

Grieve-Smith, Angus. 2009. *The Spread of Change in French Negation*. Ph.D. diss., University of New Mexico.

Hock, Hans Heinrich. 2003. Analogical Change. In *Handbook of Historical Linguistics*, ed. Brian D. Joseph and Richard D. Janda, 441–460. Oxford: Basil Blackwell.

Hooper, Joan B. 1976. Word Frequency in Lexical Diffusion and the Source of Morphophonological Change. In *Current Progress in Historical Linguistics*, ed. William Christie, 95–105. Amsterdam: North Holland.

Israel, Michael. 1998. Minimizers, Maximizers and the Rhetoric of Scalar Reasoning. *Journal of Semantics* 18: 297–331.

Jespersen, Otto. 1917. *Negation in English and Other Languages*. Copenhagen: Munksgaard.

Kroch, Anthony. 1982. *Grammatical Theory and the Quantitative Study of Syntactic Change*. Paper presented at New Ways of Analyzing Variation (NWAVE), Georgetown University.

———. 1989. Reflexes of Grammar in Patterns of Language Change. *Language Variation and Change* 1: 199–244.

Labov, William. 1972. Some Principles of Linguistic Methodology. *Language in Society* 1: 97–120.

Lotka, Alfred J. 1925. *Elements of Physical Biology*. Baltimore: Williams and Wilkins.

Lüdtke, Helmut. 1979. Auf dem Wege zu einer Theorie des Sprachwandels. In Lüdtke, Helmut, ed. *Kommunikationstheoretische Grundlagen des Sprachwandels*, p. 182–252.

Martineau, France, and Raymond Mougeon. 2003. A Sociolinguistic Study of the Origins of ne Deletion in European and Quebec French. *Language* 79: 118–152.

Maupas, Charles, père. 1607. *Grammaire et syntaxe françoise*. Rouen: Cailioue.

Malthus, Thomas. 1789. *An Essay on the Principle of Population*. London: J. Johnson.

Meillet, Antoine. 1912. L'évolution des formes grammaticales. *Scientia* 12: 384.

Offord, Malcolm. 1976. Negation in Berinus: A Contribution to the Study of Negation in Fourteenth-Century French. *Zeitschrift für romanische Philologie* 92: 313–385.

Osgood, Charles Egerton, and Thomas Albert Sebeok. 1954. Psycholinguistics: A Survey of Theory and Research Problems. *Journal of Abnormal Psychology* 49: 1–203.

Price, Glanville. 1997. Negative Particles in French. De mot en mot. In *Aspects of Medieval Linguistics*, ed. Stewart Gregory and D.A. Trotter, 173–190. Cardiff: University of Wales Press.

Schwegler, Armin. 1988. Word-Order Changes in Predicate Negation Strategies in Romance Languages. *Diachronica* 5: 21–58.

Schweighäuser, Alfred. 1852. *De la négation dans les langues romanes: Du midi et du nord de la France*. Bibliothèque de l'Ecole des Chartes, 203–247.

Schwenter, Scott A. 2006. Fine-Tuning Jespersen's Cycle. In *Drawing the Boundaries of Meaning*, ed. Betty J. Birner and Gregory Ward, 327–344. Amsterdam: John Benjamins.

Traugott, Elizabeth Closs. 1989. On the Rise of Epistemic Meanings in English: An Example of Subjectification in Semantic Change. *Language* 65: 31–55.

Vaugelas, Claude Favre de. 1647. Remarques sur la langue françoise. Paris: Augustin Courbe.

Verhulst, Pierre-François. 1838. Notice sur la loi que la population suit dans son accroissement. *Correspondence Mathématiques et Physiques* 10: 113.

Volterra, Vito. 1926. Fluctuations in the Abundance of a Species Considered Mathematically. *Nature* 118: 558–560.

Zanuttini, Raffaella. 1997. *Negation and Clausal Structure: A Comparative Study of Romance Languages*. Oxford: Oxford.

Zager, David. 1981. *A Real-Time Process Model of Morphological Change*. Buffalo: State University of New York Dissertation.

CHAPTER 6

Case Study 2: Left and Right Dislocation

Abstract Left and right dislocation were identified by Bally (1921) as "one of the most striking characteristics of spoken-language syntax." Types of dislocation include demonstrative dislocation, clitic dislocation and contrastive topics. We also find constructions that resemble dislocation, such as complex inversion and conjoined noun phrases. Grieve-Smith (Topicalization and Word Order in Conversational French. Southeast Conference on Linguistics, 2000) found that dislocation constructions were less frequent in François's (*Français parlé*. Paris: SELAF, 1974) conversational corpus than in a 1999 IRC corpus, and much less frequent in a literary magazine article. They are also less frequent in the Digital Parisian Stage corpus, and even less frequent in the 1800–1815 theatrical texts in FRANTEXT. This corroborates the evidence in Case Study 1 that FRANTEXT plays are more conservative than the average Parisian play from the same time.

Keywords Left dislocation; Right dislocation; Contrastive topic; Left detachment; French

Dislocation constructions are another phenomenon that has attracted significant attention in syntax, in French and many other languages. "Left dislocation" refers to a construction where a constituent within a sentence (the dislocated constituent) is spoken or written before the rest of the

© The Author(s) 2019

A. Grieve-Smith, *Building a Representative Theater Corpus*,
https://doi.org/10.1007/978-3-030-32402-5_6

sentence, often with some form of intonational or punctuational separation after the dislocated constituent, and an anaphoric constituent that is coreferential with the dislocated constituent. In French, *dislocation des membres de phrase* was identified by Bally (1921: §285) as "one of the most striking characteristics of spoken-language syntax."

6.1   DISLOCATIONS IN FRENCH AND OTHER LANGUAGES

Coveney (2005) writes, "Linguists have used a bewildering range of names for this and related structures." The terms "left dislocation" and "right dislocation" imply two problematic assumptions. The first is that left-to-right Roman alphabetic writing is the primary, neutral way to look at word order and sentence structure. The second is that dislocated sentences are the product of a process that transforms them from canonical sentences. Other terms that have been used are left and right "detachment," which suffer from the exact same problems as left and right dislocation, but whose metaphor is more opaque. "Topic" (see, e.g., Li and Thompson 1976) and "antitopic" (Chafe 1976) have their own problematic assumptions, namely that these constructions all serve as topic-announcing expressions. The term "topic" is also used for a dozen other, overlapping concepts (Lambrecht 1994 helps to clear up some of the confusion). Despite its problems I will use "left dislocation" here because it is a well-known, purely syntactic description. This is not to be interpreted as privileging left-to-right writing systems or derivational analyses.

6.2   PROTOTYPICAL DISLOCATIONS

There is some disagreement about what is and is not left dislocation, but there are a few forms that everyone seems to agree on as members of the category. In one form, called "hanging topic left dislocation" by Anagnostopoulou, van Riemsdijk and Zwarts (1997), a noun phrase is produced immediately before a sentence without any other syntactic connection to the sentence structure, and that sentence then has a lexical pronoun in direct object position that anaphorically refers to the dislocated noun phrase, as in this invented Dutch example:

1. *Die man, ik ken hem niet.*
   That man, I don't know him.
   (Vat 1980 [1997]: 70)

Another phenomenon, with the functionally leading name of contrastive left dislocation (van Riemsdijk 1997), occurs in verb-second Germanic languages, where the anaphoric constituent is a demonstrative pronoun and immediately follows the left dislocated constituent, as in the following example, also invented in Dutch:

2. *Die man, die ken ik niet.*
   That man, that one I don't know.
   (Vat 1980: 70)

In modern French, lexical pronouns like *lui, elle, eux* and *elles* are not typically included in the argument structure of the sentence, and thus are ineligible to take the role of anaphoric pronoun in left dislocation constructions. As a result, I have found no evidence of hanging topic left dislocation in French; instead, the anaphoric pronouns are most commonly clitic pronouns, forming "clitic left dislocation" (Cinque 1981), and the corresponding clitic right dislocation, as in the following examples:

3. MAD. VERSEUIL: *Ce d'Héricourt, un rien l'arrête, l'embarrasse* .... (Les Mœurs du jour, an VIII)
   MAD. VERSEUIL: This d'Héricourt, a tiny thing stops him, embarrasses him ....
4. GERVAULT: *Eh ! bien, voisine; nous les marions donc enfin, ces chers enfans.* (Les Tracasseries, 1804)
   GERVAULT: Well, neighbor, we're finally going to see them married, these sweet children.

In French it is also possible for the anaphoric constituent to be a demonstrative pronoun like *cela*, as in the following example. This resembles what is often called "contrastive" left dislocation, but it is not restricted to contrastive contexts. We can call it simply "demonstrative dislocation."

5. GERVAULT: *mais arroser en plein midi, cela ne vaut rien.*
   (Les Tracasseries, 1804)
   GERVAULT: but watering in the middle of the afternoon, that doesn't do anything.

Different languages allow different possibilities for the structural position of the anaphoric constituents. For example, in Italian the anaphoric constituent is never a subject (Duranti and Ochs 1979: 380–381), while in Indonesian the anaphoric constituent is never anything but the subject (Li and Thompson 1976: 470–471). In French, in addition to direct object position, the anaphoric constituents in clitic dislocations can be subject, indirect object or certain objects of the prepositions *à* and *de*, as in example (5) and the following examples:

6. TATILLON: *Un mariage d'inclination, qui finit des procès, qui assoupit des querelles, c'est touchant.* (Les Tracasseries, 1804)
     TATILLON: A marriage of love that brings the court proceedings to an end, that puts the quarrels to bed, that's touching.
7. JOCRISSE-MAITRE: *Oui, je veux te l'montrer à toi, parsque t'as du taque ….* (Jocrisse-Maître et Jocrisse-Valet, 1810)
     JOCRISSE-MAITRE: Yes, I want to show it to you, because you have some tact ….
8. MAD. EULER: *Ce cher original, songez-y, je vous prie ….* (Les Mœurs du jour, an VIII)
     MAD. EULER: That dear original, think of her, please ….

6.3   Things That Are Not Dislocations

There are some constructions that resemble dislocations, but have been shown to be syntactically and pragmatically distinct. The "complex inversion" construction noted by Kayne (1972) is one. Subject-verb inversion constructions are used to indicate questions, among other things, in French. In Old French the subjects in these constructions could be either pronouns or full noun phrases, but in Modern French they are almost exclusively produced with pronominal subjects. Today if a French speaker wants to produce a question with a full noun phrase for a subject, they will typically use either the *est-ce que* construction or an interrogative intonation contour, but in early Modern French it was common to produce the full NP immediately followed by the verb inverted with a pronominal subject, as in example (9).

9. CHARLES: *le monde n'est-il pas une loterie?* (*La Jeunesse de Favart*, 1808)
     CHARLES: The world is it not a lottery?

Following Rizzi and Roberts (1989), we can demonstrate that complex inversion is not a form of dislocation by inventing sentences with subjects that are not generally found in dislocated constituents, such as negative pronouns and noun phrases with WH-adjectives. These sentences are typically judged to be grammatical. There appears to be a change in progress from complex inversion to *est-ce que*, which is an interesting topic for another study.

Similar to complex inversion, constituents dislocated with *même* are not always syntactically separate from the main sentence, as in example (10):

10. M. MORAND: *Oui, je perds **moi-même** dans l'instant,*
    Non pas deux cents louis, ma nièce, mais deux mille. (Les Mœurs du jour, an VIII)
    M. MORAND: Yes, I myself just lost not two hundred louis, my niece, but two thousand.

Another phenomenon that resembles left dislocation is produced with conjoined noun phrases in the first and second person. These are typically produced in a dislocated position, either before or after the sentence, as in example (11). The anaphoric constituent is most frequently a plural pronoun, but may also be a quantifier like *tout*, as in example (12). They also appear to be a different type of construction from left and right dislocation.

11. TATILLON: *ne vous disputez pas trop pendant mon absence, **ma femme ou moi nous** vous aurons bientôt réconciliés.*
    (Les Tracasseries, 1804)
    TATILLON: Don't fight too much while I'm away; my wife or I will have you reconciled in no time.
12. FORMONT: *Frère, sœur, neveu, nièce, elle a **tout** oublié.*
    (Les Mœurs du jour, an VIII)
    FORMONT: Brother, sister, nephew, niece, she has forgotten it all.

6.4   SUBTYPES OF DISLOCATIONS

Lambrecht (1994) distinguishes "contrastive topics" as a subset of dislocation constructions. He writes that "the left-detachment construction is often used to mark a shift in attention from one to another of two or more already active topic referents." Because these are active referents, the dislocation is most frequently an oblique pronoun:

13. FORMONT: *Lorque la foule enfin aura pu s'écouler,*
    Je reverrai ma sœur, car je veux lui parler,
    Mais lui parler en frère, en ami vrai, fidèle.
    MAD. EULER: *Bon: **moi**, **je** vais l'attendre et fixer avec elle*
    L'heure de ce dessin, si long-tems différé;
    (Les Mœurs du jour, an VIII)
    FORMONT: Once the crowd has drifted away
    I will see my sister, for I wish to speak with her
    But to speak to her as a brother, as a true, faithful friend.
    MAD. EULER: Good. I myself will wait for her to set
    The time for this drawing session, put off for so long;

In this example, Formont tells Madame Euler that when his sister Madame Dirval returns from a ball, he intends to speak with her. Madame Euler responds by telling him that she intends to arrange a portrait sitting with Madame Dirval. Both conversational participants are automatically active referents in the discourse, and Madame Euler uses this pronominal left dislocation to shift the topic from Formont to herself. In the Digital Parisian Stage corpus the most frequent dislocated pronoun by far is *moi* (on average in 67% of left dislocated pronouns and 31% of right dislocated pronouns), potentially indicating that in these plays it is common for characters to highlight contrasts between themselves and others.

In the previous section I discussed constituents with *même*, and sentences with subject-verb inversion, which pattern in similar ways to left and right dislocation, but differ in important ways. However there are some examples with *même*, some with subject-verb inversion, and some even with both, that are clearly left dislocations, and even contrastive topics, as in example (14):

14. D'HERICOURT: *Mais vraiment,*
    ***Vous-même qui parlez**, qu'êtes-**vous** devenue?*
    (Les Mœurs du jour, an VIII)
    D'HERICOURT: But truly,
    You who speak now, what has become of you?

Contrastive topics are also possible when the topics are members of a finite list, as in example (15):

15. NICAISE: *Il y a un remède pour les biscuits qui ne sont pas empoison-nés et un autre remède pour les biscuits qui sont empoisonnés,* **celui** **pour les biscuits empoisonnés,** *je ne* **le** *connais pas.*

FLANCHET: *Dans ce cas voyos l'autre.*

NICAISE: **Celui pour les biscuits qui ne sont pas empoisonnés** *... C'est de donner vingt coups de bâton au gourmant qui les a mangé, afin qu'il n'y retourne plus.*

FLANCHET: *Je ne veux pas de ce remède.*

(*L'Absinthe*, 1805)

NICAISE: There is one remedy for cookies that have not been poisoned, and another remedy for cookies that have been poisoned. The one for poisoned cookies, I don't know it.

FLANCHET: Well then let's hear the other one.

NICAISE: The one for cookies that have not been poisoned. ... It is to give twenty whacks with a stick to the glutton who ate them, so that he does not return.

FLANCHET: I do not want that remedy.

In French the dislocated constituent can be a full noun phrase or an infinitival complement (as in the example above with *arroser*). It also includes prepositional phrases, noun phrases modified by sentential complements and sentences nominalized with complementizers, as in the following examples.

16. MAURICE: *Mais,* **c't'amour dont je m'plains, qui m'a rendu si** **tendre.** *... Qui l'a fait naître, en moi?*

(Le Singulier mariage, an IX)

MAURICE: But this love of which I complain, which has made me so sensitive. ... Who gave it life in me?

17. GERVAULT: *Tu ne sais pas?* **cette madame Lambert qui est venue** **me voir,** *ne prétend-t-elle pas que ce monsieur Tatillon lui fait la cour!*

(Les Tracasseries, 1804)

GERVAULT: You didn't know? This Madame Lambert who came to see me, she says that Monsieur Tatillon is courting her!

18. GUIGNOLET: *Ah ça, mais! c'est ti ben vrai* **ce que vous dites-là?** (Nitouche et Guignolet, an X)

GUIGNOLET: Ah, that, well! Is that really true, what you say there?

Note that in examples (16) and (18) we have interrogatives, and in example (17) we have subject-verb inversion, but they are clearly not the same phenomenon as the complex inversion identified by Kayne (1972). It is important to distinguish them clearly.

French also has instances where the dislocated constituent is marked by a preposition that specifically indicates a topic-announcing expression, as in the following examples:

19. MAD. EULER: ***Pour moi**, je serai bientôt prête*;
    (Les Mœurs du jour, an VIII)
    MAD. EULER: Well, **I** will be ready soon.
20. HORTENCE: ***Quant à Nicaise et Jeannette**, je **leur** rends ma parole et toute mon amitié* .... (L'Absinthe, 1805)
    HORTENCE: And as for Nicaise and Jeannette, I restore to them my trust and all my esteem ....

The following table (Table 6.1) summarizes dislocation-related phenomena.

6.5   DISLOCATION CONSTRUCTIONS AND TOPIC PROMINENCE

As suggested by their alternate names, "topic" and "antitopic," dislocation constructions serve to communicate information structure (Lambrecht 1994). In French, in particular, dislocation constructions with full noun phrases often serve as topic-announcing expressions. In example (3) the phrase "*ce d'Héricourt*" serves to promote the character d'Héricourt to the topic of the sentence, in fact the topic of an entire short soliloquy, and the rest of the sentence comments on him. In example (4) "*ces chers enfants*" serves to indicate that it was the (adult) children who were to be married.

Li and Thompson (1976) categorize languages as topic-prominent (which they abbreviate Tp) and subject-prominent types. In topic-prominent languages like Mandarin Chinese and the Lolo-Burmese language Lahu, the canonical sentence structure includes a topic-announcing expression and an expression commenting on that topic. In subject-prominent languages like English and Indonesian, the canonical sentence structure includes a predicate and an expression that highlights the agent or experiencer of that predicate. In this typology it is also possible for languages to be both topic-prominent

Table 6.1 Types of left dislocation and other constructions that resemble left dislocation

Name	Necessary condition	Alternative names	Found in French	Included as dislocation
Hanging topic left dislocation	Lexical anaphoric pronoun	HTLD, left dislocation, left detachment, topic	No	Yes
Demonstrative dislocation	Demonstrative anaphoric pronoun	Contrastive left/right dislocation, CLD/CRD	Yes	Yes
Clitic left/right dislocation	Clitic anaphoric pronoun	CLLD/CLRD, topic/antitopic, subject doubling, reprise	Yes	Yes
Contrastive topic/antitopic	Clitic anaphoric pronoun, dislocated oblique pronoun	Subject doubling	Yes	Yes
Prepositional topic-announcing expression	Preposition like *pour* or *quant à*		Yes	Yes
Complex inversion	Inverted subject and verb; dislocated constituent is coreferential with subject pronoun	CI	Yes	No
Conjoined noun phrases	Plural anaphoric pronoun, coreferential with conjoined dislocated constituent	CNP	Yes	No
Même phrase	Dislocated constituent suffixed with *même*		Yes	No

and subject-prominent (Li and Thompson give Japanese and Korean as examples) or neither (Tagalog and Ilocano). They further propose that languages may evolve on a path from topic-prominent to neither, and then to subject-prominent, to both, and back to topic-prominent.

In a conference paper, "Topicalization and word order in conversational French" (Grieve-Smith 2000) I addressed the possibility that the use of these topic-announcing expressions in French could be evidence of topic-prominent qualities in the language. Li and Thompson (1976: 466–471) list eight characteristics of topic-prominent languages, but they are not working from a representative corpus, so the characteristics they give are all binary, existential observations: Does the language have a passive construction? Are there constraints on what can appear in the topic construction?

In the Topicalization study I built on Li and Thompson's observations by devising quantitative, corpus-based tests for three of these characteristics (use of the passive construction, "dummy" subjects and verb-final word order). It would also be possible to develop tests for three others ("double subject" constructions, controlling co-reference and constraints on the topic constituent) in the future.

For the Topicalization study I decided to replace Li and Thompson's (1976) two other binary characteristics with quantitative measures. Li and Thompson's characteristic (a) is the simple existence of surface coding for topic-announcing expressions, and the use of left and right dislocations both satisfy that criterion, while (h) is the "basicness of topic-comment sentences." The answers to these questions are simple: yes, left and right dislocation do exist in French, but no, they do not follow the patterns demonstrated by Li and Thompson for topic-comment constructions in Lisu and Mandarin.

To create a quantitative measure similar to the existence and basicness of topic-announcing constructions I tested the token frequency of left and right dislocations in French, as a proportion of the total number of sentences in a text. At that stage of the investigation I was not aware of the distinctions between clitic left dislocation, contrastive topics, conjoined noun phrases and complex inversion, so I counted them all as "topics."

I measured these frequencies in two small, not particularly representative corpora. The first was the transcript of several hours of casual face-to-face conversation recorded by François (1974) in her family home in Argenteuil in 1964. The second was a log of several hours of casual conversation on the Internet Relay Chat (IRC) public channel #france. To test Bally's (1921) observation that dislocation constructions are particularly characteristic of spoken language, I added a recent magazine article of literary criticism (Sollers 1999).

6.6   Left and Right Dislocation in Three Preliminary Corpora

In the Topicalization study (Grieve-Smith 2000), I found a large difference in the token frequency of left and right dislocation, as a percentage of the total number of finite clauses (Table 6.2).

Table 6.2 Left and right dislocations as a percentage of total clauses in the IRC, François and literary corpora, from Grieve-Smith (2000)

Participant	Corpus	LD	RD	Clauses	LD (%)	RD (%)
Chipie	IRC	13	13	149	8.72	8.72
e2	IRC	26	10	92	28.26	10.87
Nougat	IRC	17	15	131	12.98	11.45
titepuce	IRC	6	15	98	6.12	15.31
Yield_	IRC	4	8	47	8.51	17.02
Average	IRC	66	61	517	12.92	12.67
LS	François	20	0	252	7.94	0.00
Sollers	Livres	1	0	47	2.13	0.00

In François (1974), the speaker LS is 65 years old at the time of recording in 1964, meaning that he was born in 1898 or 1899. The IRC chatters were all in their teens or early twenties when they participated in those chats in 1999–2000, which puts their birth years in the late 1970s and early 1980s. In apparent time (Labov 1963) this makes for a difference of almost 80 years. Philippe Sollers was born in 1936.

We do not have evidence that any of these texts are representative of a larger group, but if they are it would suggest three things: (a) Bally (1921) may be correct and spoken conversational French has a much higher use of left and right dislocations than formal written French, (b) written conversational chat may be more like spoken conversation than like written literary magazine articles, and (c) the frequency of dislocations in conversational French may be rising.

Without a detailed study of representative corpora we cannot tell for certain, but a rise in frequency may indicate that there is ongoing analogical extension of dislocation constructions, similar to the extension that may be occurring for *ne ... pas*. Such an extension may be part of a shift to greater topic prominence of the type described by Li and Thompson (1976).

6.7   Dislocation Constructions in FRANTEXT and the Digital Parisian Stage

As I read through the Digital Parisian Stage texts for the study of negation in Chap. 5 I noticed that some characters produced left and right dislocations at a fairly high rate, and I had the impression that these were the same characters who tended to use *ne ... pas* more frequently. It may be that a similar social dynamic is at work.

Table 6.3 Left and right dislocation in FRANTEXT and the Digital Parisian Stage (both 1800–1815) compared to the three corpora consulted in the Topicalization study (Grieve-Smith 2000)

Corpus	LD	RD	Clauses	LD (%)	RD (%)
FRANTEXT	115	31	7606	1.55	0.428
Digital Parisian Stage	390	152	17,704	2.11	0.911
Livres (Sollers 1999)	1	0	47	2.13	0.00
François (1974)	20	0	252	7.94	0.00
IRC corpus	66	61	517	12.92	12.67

To confirm this impression, I annotated all instances of left and right dislocation in the Digital Parisian Stage corpus (excluding *la Mort du Capitaine Cook* as in Chap. 7) and in the four FRANTEXT plays. I used the AnnotatorJS library with tags and a custom data store (Grieve-Smith 2018) to mark the dislocation constructions.

Given the different types of dislocations and similar constructions that I described in previous sections, I tagged demonstrative dislocation, complex inversion, contrastive topic, conjoined noun phrases and constructions with prepositions like *pour* and *quant à*. I excluded constructions with *-même* unless they were clearly intended to announce a topic. Full tables are in the Appendices.

The data is summarized in the following tables. Table 6.3 combines all left dislocation and similar constructions, for comparison with the corpora I examined in the Topicalization study (Grieve-Smith 2000).

The data are drawn from several different genres and registers, and some are not representative samples at all. However, they suggest that if in the future we establish a diachronic corpus based on representative samples of comparable registers and genres, we are likely to find both an increase over time and an effect of genre and register.

6.8   Left Dislocation Constructions in the Two Corpora

If we separate the quasi-left dislocations in FRANTEXT and the Digital Parisian Stage corpus into the types of left dislocations I discussed above (clitic left dislocation, demonstrative left dislocation, contrastive topics and prepositional topic-announcing expressions) and similar constructions (complex inversion, conjoined noun phrases and *même* pronominals),

Table 6.4 Left dislocations and similar constructions in FRANTEXT and the Digital Parisian Stage, as a percentage of all sentences

Feature	FRANTEXT	DPS	FRANTEXT (%)	DPS (%)	p	d
Complex inversion	41	92	0.561	0.615	0.691	0.0908
Contrastive topics	19	161	0.238	0.760	**0.000160**	**1.04**
Prepositional topic-announcing expression	4	26	0.0390	0.117	0.061	0.449
Conjoined noun phrase	3	4	0.0396	0.0249	0.391	−0.197
Clitic left dislocation	41	119	0.572	0.633	0.627	0.112
Demonstrative left dislocation	1	19	0.00903	0.113	**0.0163**	**0.595**
Total quasi-left dislocations	115	391	1.55	2.11	**0.0295**	**0.527**

how do the two corpora differ? How do these constructions compare to each other? Table 6.4 lists the raw token frequencies and the percentage of all sentences for each of these constructions, and the results of Student's *t*-test and Cohen's *d* measure of effect size for the differences in percentages between the two corpora.

Prepositional topic-announcing expressions (those with *quant à* and *pour*) pattern with the other left dislocations, with no significant difference between FRANTEXT and the Digital Parisian Stage. This suggests that they should be grouped in with the other left dislocations.

Complex inversions and conjoined noun phrases have no significant difference in frequency between FRANTEXT and the Digital Parisian stage. Conjoined noun phrases are also low in frequency in both corpora. This suggests that both of these constructions can be excluded from the rest of this study.

I was somewhat surprised to find no significant difference between FRANTEXT (0.572%) and the Digital Parisian Stage (0.633%) in clitic left dislocation (excluding contrastive topics). The difference between the two corpora in the frequency of demonstrative left dislocation (also known as contrastive left dislocation) is significant, and the effect size is moderate ($d = 0.595$), but this construction is very infrequent (it is used in 0.113% of sentences in the Digital Parisian Stage) compared to clitic left dislocation (used in 0.633% of sentences). The primary significant difference

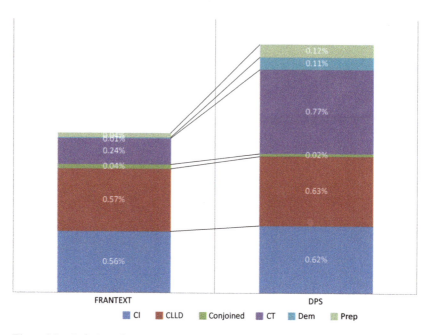

Fig. 6.1 Relative frequencies of left dislocation-related constructions in FRANTEXT and the Digital Parisian Stage

between the two corpora was in the frequency of contrastive topic-announcing expressions. This also had a large effect size ($d > 0.8$). Contrastive topics are primarily responsible for the difference in frequency of left dislocation and similar constructions, as illustrated by Fig. 6.1.

If there is a shift to more dislocations in progress in the early nineteenth century, as suggested by the diachronic data in Table 6.3, it is likely that any increase in non-contrastive dislocations was largely complete before the beginning of the nineteenth century, and that the increase in left dislocations during this period was due to increased use of contrastive topic-announcing expressions.

6.9   Right Dislocation Constructions in the Two Corpora

Each of the constructions we have discussed in French in this chapter occurs in both left (preceding the sentence) and right (following the sentence) forms. In the nineteenth-century corpora the post-sentence forms

Table 6.5 Right dislocations and similar constructions in FRANTEXT and the Digital Parisian Stage, as a percentage of all sentences

Feature	FRANTEXT	DPS	FRANTEXT (%)	DPS (%)	p	d
Total quasi-right dislocations	31	152	0.428	0.912	**0.0108**	**0.627**
Complex inversion	1	3	0.0202	0.0172	0.774	−0.0632
Contrastive antitopics	19	64	0.227	0.417	0.187	0.308
Prepositional topic-announcing expression	1	2	0.0202	0.144	0.572	−0.125
Conjoined noun phrase	3	4	0.0271	0.0168	0.305	−0.219
Clitic right dislocation	5	67	0.0918	0.420	**0.0000600**	**1.13**
Demonstrative right dislocation	5	16	0.0897	0.0932	0.907	0.0247

are all less frequent than their sentence-preceding counterparts, but all occur at least once. Table 6.5 lists the frequencies, percentages and p and d values for the right-hand versions.

As with left dislocations, right dislocated prepositional topic-announcing expressions, complex inversions and conjoined noun phrases are infrequent and have no significant difference in frequency between the two corpora. This suggests that we can treat them as we did with their left dislocated counterparts: group the prepositional topic-announcing expressions with the non-prepositional right dislocations and exclude the complex inversions and conjoined noun phrases.

Unlike with left dislocations, there is no significant difference between FRANTEXT and the Digital Parisian Stage for contrastive antitopics, but the difference between the two corpora for clitic right dislocation is significant, with a large effect size ($d = 1.13$). We can see in Fig. 6.2 that clitic right dislocation is the biggest contributor to the difference between the two corpora for right dislocations and similar constructions.

The pragmatics of right and left dislocations are not identical, so it is not very surprising that there is a large increase in clitic right dislocations, but no large increase in contrastive antitopics.

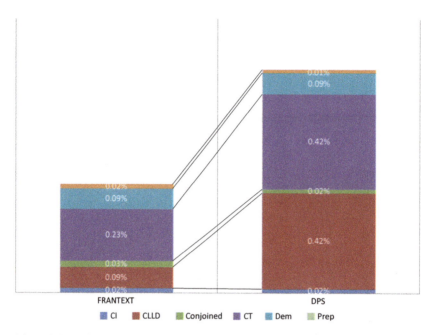

Fig. 6.2 Relative frequency of right dislocation-related constructions in FRANTEXT and the Digital Parisian Stage

REFERENCES

Anagnostopoulou, Elena, Henk van Riemsdijk, and Franz Zwarts, eds. 1997. *Materials on Left Dislocation*. Amsterdam: John Benjamins.

Bally, Charles. 1921. *Traité de Stylistique Francaise*. 2nd ed. Heidelberg: Carl Winter.

Chafe, Wallace L. 1976. Givenness, Contrastiveness, Definiteness, Subjects, Topics and Points of View. In *Subject and Topic*, ed. Charles Li. New York: Academic Press.

Cinque, Guglielmo. 1981. *'Topic' Constructions in Some European Languages and 'Connectedness'*. Reprinted in Anagnostopoulou et al. 1997, pages 93–118.

Coveney, Aidan. 2005. Subject Doubling in Spoken French: A Sociolinguistic Approach. *The French Review* 79: 1.

Duranti, Alessandro, and Elinor Ochs. 1979. Left-Dislocation in Italian Conversation. In *Syntax and Semantics 12: Discourse and Syntax*, ed. Talmy Givón. New York: Academic Press.

François, Denise. 1974. *Français parlé*. Paris: SELAF.

Grieve-Smith, Angus. 2000. Topicalization and Word Order in Conversational French. Southeast Conference on Linguistics.

Grieve-Smith, Angus. 2018. Annotation: U store it. Modern Language Association.

Kayne, Richard. 1972. Subject Inversion in French Interrogatives. In *Generative Studies in Romance Languages*, ed. J. Casagrande and B. Saciuk, 70–126. Rowley, MA: Newbury House.

Labov, William. 1963. The Social Motivation of a Sound Change. *WORD* 19 (3): 273–309.

Lambrecht, Knud. 1994. *Information Structure and Sentence Form: Topic, Focus, and the Mental Representations of Discourse Referents*. Cambridge: Cambridge University Press.

Li, Charles, and Sandra Thompson. 1976. Subject and Topic: A New Typology of Language. In *Subject and Topic*, ed. Charles Li. New York: Academic Press.

van Riemsdijk, Henk. 1997. Left Dislocation. In Anagnostopoulou et al. 1997, pages 1–10.

Rizzi, Luigi, and Ian Roberts. 1989. Complex Inversion in French. *Probus* 1: 1.

Sollers, Philippe. 1999. La société de Balzac. Le monde des livres.

Vat, Jan. 1980. *Left Dislocation, Connectedness and Reconstruction*. Reprinted in Anagnostopoulou et al. 1997, pages 67–92.

CHAPTER 7

Social Factors in Building a Theater Corpus

Abstract The two case studies in this book found significant syntactic differences in between FRANTEXT and the Digital Parisian Stage corpus, with large effect sizes. Are these differences due to social biases in the choice of theatrical texts for FRANTEXT, or the lack of availability of certain texts in the Digital Parisian Stage sample? When examined with one-way analysis of variation (ANOVA), differences in negation proved to have a significant relationship to both the genre of the play and the theater where it premièred. No significant relationship was found between differences in dislocation frequency and genre or theater, or between any of the linguistic variables and factors like gender, age and social class. A larger sample may indicate such relationships beyond the possibility of sampling error.

Keywords Genre; Theater; French; Negation; Dislocation

In the previous chapters we have seen significant differences between FRANTEXT and the randomly sampled Digital Parisian Stage corpus, with large effect sizes, for the relative token frequencies of *ne ... pas*, contrastive topics, demonstrative left dislocation and clitic right dislocation. In this chapter I present an analysis that traces these differences to the different mixes of genres and theaters in the two corpora. These mixes in turn clearly

© The Author(s) 2019
A. Grieve-Smith, *Building a Representative Theater Corpus*,
https://doi.org/10.1007/978-3-030-32402-5_7

reflect the different sampling methods employed in constructing the two corpora, specifically the bias introduced by the Principle of Authority used in the compilation of FRANTEXT. I also investigate the hypothesis that these differences are due to differences in the mix of ages, genders and social classes in the two corpora.

Before we examine the social factors, it is important to consider two potential alternative sources of bias. One risk that we face with all random selection methods is that the method may have accidentally retrieved a biased sample. The tests of statistical significance I have applied to the data (Student's t-test and ANOVA) show that the risk is within an acceptable range of 1% (well within $p < 0.05$).

Another possible source of bias is in the preservation and distribution of the plays. In Chap. 3 I mentioned that there is bias in the selection of texts for publication, preservation and digital distribution. In Chap. 6 I discussed the effect of this bias: of the 31 plays randomly selected for the Digital Parisian Stage corpus, 6 were never published, and I have only been able to obtain the manuscript for one of these. The other five are summarized in Table 7.1 below:

The fact that these plays were never published is not likely to be the source of the differences. As I will demonstrate below, the frequencies of the sentence negators and dislocation constructions vary across the genres assigned to the plays and the theaters where they premièred. The five missing plays are closer to the 23 full-text plays in their genres and the theaters where they were performed than they are to the four plays in FRANTEXT. Their absence is thus more likely to have reduced the differences in negation and dislocation than it is to have increased them. I will revisit this in detail below when I discuss variation by genre and theater.

Table 7.1 The five plays in the Digital Parisian Stage corpus that are currently unavailable

Title	Genre	Theater
L'Abbaye de Grasville	*mélodrame*	TMA
Le Baron de Felsheim	*mélodrame-comique*	PSM
La Dame invisible	*vaudeville*	TMV
L'Epreuve excusable	*comédie*	TC
La Méprise	*comédie*	TF

7.1   NEGATION AND GENRE OF PLAYS

In the early-nineteenth-century Paris the genre of most plays was specified in correspondence, theater listings, newspaper reviews and scripts. There were a finite number of these genres, and Wicks (1950) lists them whenever possible. He did not list genres for 7 of the 31 listings in the corpus, but in all these cases I have been able to find them documented in other sources.

There were also a finite number of theaters, and every entry in Wicks (1950) has a theater associated with it. Some of these theater entries conflicted with information in listings or published plays; in those cases I used the listings or published plays.

Table 7.2 lists the four plays in the FRANTEXT corpus with their genres and theaters, and the frequency of sentence negators:

In terms of genre, *Cœlina* was marketed as a *drame*, but all of the literary histories I consulted (including those that were originally consulted for FRANTEXT, as well as histories of popular theater like Carlson 1972) identify it as an early and influential melodrama. The word *mélodrame* already existed, but it may be that Pixérécourt or his producers felt at the time that it was not prestigious enough. Out of over 3000 plays, Wicks (1950) identifies 276 as melodramas and only 50 as dramas. There are no plays identified as dramas in the Digital Parisian Stage sample for this period, and one melodrama.

Similarly, *La Mort de Henri IV* and *Wallstein* are described as *tragédies* on their title pages, and unlike *Cœlina*, this categorization is not disputed. *La Mort de Henri IV* is among 32 plays marked as tragedies in Wicks (1950), but *Wallstein* is not listed in *The Parisian Stage* because it

Table 7.2 Genre, theater and the relative frequencies of declarative sentence negations in the four plays in the FRANTEXT corpus (1800–1815)

Title	Genre	Theater	ne *alone* (%)	ne ... pas (%)	ne ... point (%)
Cœlina, ou L'Enfant du Mystère	*drame*	TAC	18.49	60.27	21.23
La Mort de Henri IV	*tragédie*	TF	39.36	48.94	11.70
Pinto	*comédie héroïque*	TF	27.57	52.97	19.46
Wallstein	*tragédie*	Closet	34.91	33.96	31.13
Average			28.63	50.47	20.90

Table 7.3 Average relative frequency of declarative sentence negations by genre in the Digital Parisian Stage corpus

Genre	Count	ne *alone* (%)	ne ... pas (%)	ne ... point (%)
com	8	11.87%	79.08%	9.05%
com.-vaud	2	16.18%	78.63%	5.19%
mélo	1	31.65%	30.38%	37.97%
op.	1	61.54%	23.08%	15.38%
op.-com	2	8.30%	91.70%	0.00%
parade	2	12.91%	82.55%	4.55%
pièce	1	10.34%	87.93%	1.72%
prol.	2	8.00%	58.67%	33.33%
vaud.	3	14.72%	68.10%	17.18%
$F(8,22)$		7.24	3.76	1.25
P		**0.000978**	**0.0167**	0.348
η^2		0.816	0.653	
ω^2		0.694	0.468	

was never performed. None of those 32 tragedies are in the Digital Parisian Stage sample.

Pinto is described on its title page as a *comédie historique*. There are 11 *comédies historiques* listed in Wicks (1950), but *Pinto* is listed there as one of two *com. héroïque*. None of the historical or heroic comedies are in the Digital Parisian Stage sample. *Pinto* is a historical play with a happy ending and scenes of action and intrigue; of all the plays in the Digital Parisian Stage it probably resembles most closely the melodrama *Les Strélitz*, but it also fits with some of the more serious comedies in the sample, such as *Les Mœurs du jour*.

Table 7.3 shows how negation features are distributed across genres in the Digital Parisian Stage corpus.

For *ne* alone (as opposed to the embracing negation constructions) and *ne ... pas*, a one-way analysis of variance (ANOVA, Fisher 1921) allows us to rule out the possibility that the differences between genres are due to random bias in the sample. The stacked bar chart in Fig. 7.1 shows the genres ordered by relative frequency of *ne ... pas*.

Comparing the four FRANTEXT plays with the genre averages in the Digital Parisian Stage for negation, we see that *Cœlina* and *Pinto* are close to *Les Strélitz*, the single melodrama and the second most conservative play in the Digital Parisian Stage sample. The two tragedies are more conservative than that, closer to the single opera in the sample, *Nephtali*. The other 21 plays in the Digital Parisian Stage all use more *ne ... pas* and less

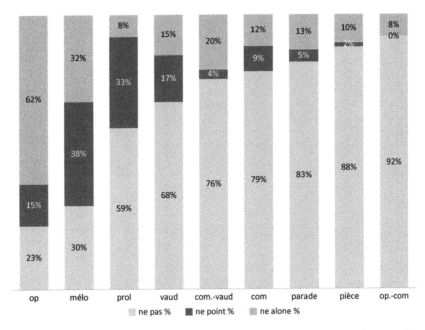

Fig. 7.1 Average relative frequency of declarative sentence negations by genre in the Digital Parisian Stage corpus, sorted by relative frequency Fig. 7.2 of *ne ... pas*

ne alone than any of the FRANTEXT plays. The bias in FRANTEXT's Principle of Authority is thus applied through the choice of genres: the theaters are showing comedies and vaudevilles, while the literary historians talk mostly about tragedies.

Of the five missing plays in the Digital Parisian Stage, the only one that shares a genre with a FRANTEXT play is the melodrama *L'Abbaye de Grasville*. The other four include two comedies, a melodrama-comedy and a vaudeville. If these plays fit with the available comedies and vaudevilles in the corpus, we would expect them all to be more innovative in negation frequencies than the FRANTEXT plays, increasing the difference between the averages of the two corpora.

7.2   Dislocation and Genre of Plays

How did the different genres pattern for left and right dislocation? Let's compare them, looking at the criteria where I found significant differences between the corpora in Chap. 6 (Table 7.4).

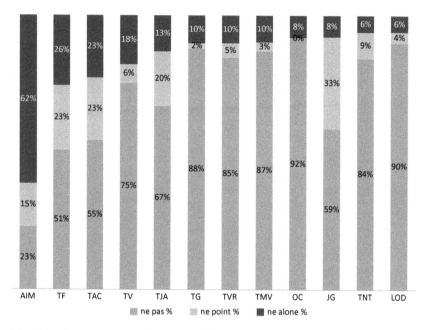

Fig. 7.2 Average relative frequency of declarative sentence negations by theater in the Digital Parisian Stage corpus, inversely sorted by relative frequency of *ne* alone

Table 7.4 Genre, theater and the relative frequencies of left and right dislocation constructions in the four plays in the FRANTEXT corpus (1800–1815)

Title	Genre	Theater	LD CT (%)	Demonstrative LD (%)	CLRD (%)
Cœlina	drame	TAC	0.161%	0	0.2419%
La Mort de Henri IV	tragédie	TF	0.251%	0	0.0836%
Pinto	comédie héroïque	TF	0.289%	0.0361%	0
Wallstein	tragédie	Closet	0.250%	0	0.0416%
Average			0.238%	0.00903	0.0918%

One-way ANOVA shows that unlike with negation, differences in the frequencies of dislocation constructions are not a significant effect of genre (Table 7.5).

Table 7.5 Average relative frequency of dislocation constructions by genre in the Digital Parisian Stage corpus

Genre	Count	LD CT (%)	Demonstrative LD (%)	CLRD (%)
com.	8	1.132%	0.157%	0.542%
com.-vaud.	2	0.880%	0.231%	0.231%
mélo.	1	0.177%	0.000%	0.355%
op.	1	0.264%	0.000%	0.528%
op.-com.	2	0.608%	0.000%	0.215%
Parade	2	0.460%	0.073%	0.230%
Pièce	1	0.548%	0.548%	0.366%
prol.	2	0.000%	0.000%	0.881%
vaud.	3	0.984%	0.027%	0.182%
$F(8,22)$		1.84	1.35	1.49
P		0.157	0.299	0.250

The differences appear to be fairly large, which suggests that a larger sample might help to rule out the possibility of a sampling error. A follow-up study with a larger sample could potentially confirm some of these patterns. This might even be possible with a 1% sample of the full nineteenth century.

7.3   Theaters of Plays in the Two Corpora

As discussed in Chap. 5, the imperial decrees of 1807 assigned genres to the licensed theaters of Paris, but even before that the theaters had specialized in particular genres. In addition, the theater directors had some control over what plays were staged in their theaters. We might therefore expect to find that negation and dislocation were expressed differently from theater to theater (Tables 7.6 and 7.7).

The relative frequency of *ne* alone (by contrast with either *ne … pas* or *ne … point*) is the only measure of either dislocation or negation where genre differences are statistically significant. The stacked bar chart in Fig. 7.2 shows the use of these negators in each theater, inversely ordered by the relative frequency of *ne* alone.

As with genre, the FRANTEXT plays are drawn from the repertoires of the more conservative theaters. *La Mort de Henri IV* and *Pinto* were performed at the Comédie-Française, the second most conservative theater for the use of *ne* alone. It is not surprising that *Wallstein*, as an elite closet drama, is even more conservative. *Cœlina* premièred at the Théâtre de l'Ambigu-Comique, the third-most conservative theater.

Table 7.6 Average relative frequency of declarative sentence negations by theater in the Digital Parisian Stage corpus

Theater	Rank	Count	ne *alone (%)*	ne pas *(%)*	ne point *(%)*
AIM	Grand	1	61.54%	23.08%	15.38%
JG	Tolerated	2	8.00%	58.67%	33.33%
LOD	Grand	1	6.19%	90.00%	3.81%
OC	Grand	2	8.30%	91.70%	0.00%
TAC	Secondary	2	22.89%	54.58%	22.52%
TF	Grand	1	25.73%	50.97%	23.30%
TG	Secondary	1	10.34%	87.93%	1.72%
TJA	Closed	3	13.33%	66.99%	19.68%
TNT	Closed	1	6.25%	84.38%	9.38%
TV	Secondary	3	18.06%	75.45%	6.49%
TVR	Secondary	5	10.16%	85.57%	4.27%
$F(10,22)$			7.38	2.21	0.819
P			**0.00136**	0.0632	0.620
η^2			0.870		
ω^2			0.744		

Table 7.7 Average relative frequency of dislocation constructions by theater in the Digital Parisian Stage corpus

Theater	Rank	Count	LD CT (%)	Demonstrative LD (%)	CLRD (%)
AIM	Grand	1	0.264%	0.0000%	0.528%
JG	Tolerated	2	0.000%	0.0000%	0.881%
LOD	Grand	1	1.288%	0.1227%	0.675%
OC	Grand	2	0.608%	0.0000%	0.215%
TAC	Secondary	2	0.379%	0.0000%	0.468%
TF	Grand	1	1.733%	0.0707%	0.248%
TG	Secondary	1	0.548%	0.5484%	0.366%
TJA	Closed	3	0.982%	0.2562%	0.583%
TNT	Closed	1	1.103%	0.0000%	0.368%
TV	Secondary	3	0.684%	0.2028%	0.203%
TVR	Secondary	5	0.997%	0.0743%	0.315%
$F(10,22)$			1.49	1.21	0.899
P			0.261	0.373	0.563

If we assume that each of the five plays that are missing from the Digital Parisian Stage sample resembled the other plays performed at the same theater, then *La Méprise* would likely be as conservative as *Pinto* because they were both performed at the Comédie-Française. *La Dame invisible* was performed at the Théâtre du Vaudeville and we would thus expect it to have moderate frequencies of *ne* alone, and *L'Epreuve excusable* was performed at the Théâtre de la Gaîté and would be as innovative as *Le Grenadier de Louis XV*. *L'Abbaye de Grasville* premièred at the Théâtre du Marais and *le Baron de Felsheim* at the Théâtre de la Porte-Saint-Martin. These last two theaters closed midway through the 1800–1815 sample period, and thus there are no plays in the sample with available full text. As with genres, therefore, we would expect the average negation frequencies to be more innovative if these five plays are found and added to the corpus.

7.4   CHARACTERISTICS OF CHARACTERS IN THE TWO CORPORA

If there are differences among these genres and theaters in negation and dislocation, they may well be due to differences in the speech of the characters in the respective plays. This may be due to actual differences in the speech of people that these characters are intended to represent, but as Lodge (1991) cautions, we cannot assume that these are faithful representations of the way people spoke at the time.

Linguists have abundantly documented the effects of age (Labov 1963), gender (Trudgill 1972) and social class (Labov 1966). It would thus be normal to find effects of these variables in the relative frequency of sentence negation. To test this I identified the character in each play who produced the largest number of sentences. It is possible to separate the speech of every character in each corpus and look for effects of social class, age and gender. This would introduce two potential confounding factors. First, it is well documented (Giles and Smith 1979) that people have a tendency to accommodate their speech to that of their interlocutors. Secondly, the characters in each play are the product of a single playwright or team of playwrights, sometimes in conjunction with an acting troupe. While most playwrights and players are clearly able to differentiate the speech of their characters within a given play, they may also impose stylistic uniformities that are not typical of spontaneous speech. It would be possible to test and compensate for these confounding factors in a follow-up analysis. For this study I chose to measure only the character with the highest sentence count in each play.

Of these characters, only one was below adult age: Félix, the leader of the titular *Petits Braconniers*, who I classified as a Teen. I classified some as Elderly because they were described as *vieille* "old" in the dramatis personae

Table 7.8 Effects of character age on the relative frequency of constructions for declarative sentence negation and dislocation in the Digital Parisian Stage corpus

Age	Number of characters	ne *alone* (%)	ne … pas (%)	ne … point (%)	LD CT (%)	Demonstrative LD (%)	CLRD (%)
Adult	9	23.73%	66.27%	10.00%	0.55%	0.10%	0.44%
Elderly	3	12.45%	77.84%	9.71%	0.33%	0.00%	0.10%
Teen	1	0.00%	100.00%	0.00%	1.18%	0.00%	0.00%
Young adult	9	13.40%	80.95%	5.65%	1.15%	0.18%	0.81%
F		1.56	1.26	0.429	0.956	0.418	1.435
p		0.233	0.316	0.734	0.434	0.742	0.265

Table 7.9 Effects of character gender on the relative frequency of constructions for declarative sentence negation and dislocation in the Digital Parisian Stage corpus

Gender	Number of characters	ne *alone* (%)	ne … pas (%)	ne … point (%)	LD CT (%)	Demonstrative LD (%)	CLRD (%)
Men	19	14.61%	75.06%	10.33%	0.872%	0.138%	0.427%
Women	4	14.64%	78.15%	7.20%	0.415%	0.029%	0.398%
p		0.993	0.676	0.600	0.0828	0.0743	0.850

(Marcelline), had adult children (Maria) or took a parental role toward young adults (Hortence). Several characters were described as *jeune* "young" (Sainville, Guignolet), or were newlyweds (Jocrisse-Maître), employed bourgeois living with their parents (Charles, Piron) or subjects of marriage plots where their age was unremarked (Jacques, Suzette), and therefore were classified as Young Adults. The rest were classified as Adults (Table 7.8).

There were no explicitly gender variant or genderfluid characters, and the gender roles of the characters were often central to the plots. In *Papirius*, Calphurnie is the leader of an uprising of patrician women, and in *Les Mœurs du jour*, Formont's status as the older brother of Madame Dirval enables him to protect her from predatory men while her husband is at war. As is normal for French, every one of these characters was referred to with explicitly gendered pronouns and adjectives, which made them easy to classify according to the intentions of the playwrights (Table 7.9).

Table 7.10 Effects of character social class on the relative frequency of constructions for declarative sentence negation and dislocation in the Digital Parisian Stage corpus

Class	Number of characters	ne alone (%)	ne ... pas (%)	ne ... point (%)	LD CT (%)	Demonstrative LD (%)	CLRD (%)
Bourgeois	6	12.7%	80.2%	7.04%	0.878%	0.0748%	0.289%
Doméstique	3	11.7%	78.5%	9.82%	1.21%	0.352%	0.675%
Noble	6	21.1%	57.3%	21.5%	0.346%	0.0243%	0.402%
Paysan	3	14.7%	73.5%	11.8%	0.756%	0.0485%	0.639%
Propriétaire	4	12.7%	80.1%	7.21%	0.928%	0.206%	0.288%
F		0.434	1.19	0.736	1.74	2.42	1.46
P		0.783	0.350	0.580	0.186	0.0876	0.258

To examine social class I took the occupational, family and class information provided in the dramatis personae of each play. Their individual negation usage is reported in the Appendices. Some (Maria, Calphurnie) were described with explicit ranks as belonging to the nobility. Others were identified as domestic servants or slaves (Jacques, Esope). With the servants I also included Jocrisse-Maître, who had lived as a servant for all his life until just before the start of the play. There were characters who were explicitly described as peasants (Guignolet, Zimeline) or farm boys (Maurice). I divided the remaining characters into rural landowners (*propriétaires*, like Formont and La Grenade) and urban *bourgeois* (either Parisians in Paris like Charles Favart, or Parisians visiting the country like Sainville). Among the rural landowners I included Monsieur Tatillon because he successfully passes for a prosperous villager, despite not owning any property (Table 7.10).

There appear to be patterns in the data, but they are not strong enough to rule out the possibility of sampling error. As with genre, a follow-up study with a larger sample could potentially confirm some of these patterns.

REFERENCES

Carlson, Marvin. 1972. *The French Stage in the Nineteenth Century*. Metuchen: Scarecrow.

Fisher, Ronald. 1921. On the "Probable Error" of a Coefficient of Correlation Deduced from a Small Sample. *Metron* 1 (1): 3–32.

Giles, Howard, and Philip Smith. 1979. Accommodation Theory: Optimal Levels of Convergence. In *Language and Social Psychology*, ed. Howard Giles and Robert N. St. Clair. Baltimore: Basil Blackwell.

Labov, William. 1963. The Social Motivation of a Sound Change. *WORD* 19 (3): 273–309.

———. 1966. *The Social Stratification of English in New York City*. Washington, DC: Center for Applied Linguistics.

Lodge, Anthony. 1991. Molière's Peasants and the Norms of Spoken French. *Neuphilologische Mitteilungen* 92: 485–499.

Trudgill, Peter. 1972. Sex, Covert Prestige and Linguistic Change in the Urban British English of Norwich. *Language in Society* 1: 2.

Wicks, Charles Beaumont. 1950, 1953, 1961, 1967, 1979. *The Parisian Stage*. Tuscaloosa: University of Alabama.

CHAPTER 8

Conclusion

Abstract The Digital Parisian Stage project offers a much more representative picture of the language of Parisian theater than any known corpus of
the same period. Work is continuing on Part II of the project; when the
corpus is complete it will provide a more reliable sample for historical
studies of the French language.

Keywords French; Theater; Corpus; Sample; Nineteenth century

The primary inspiration for the Digital Parisian Stage corpus was my dissertation study, *The Spread of Change in French Negation* (Grieve-Smith
2009). One of the major assumptions underlying that study was that the
texts in FRANTEXT for one period are representative of the language
input for authors who wrote the texts in FRANTEXT in a subsequent
period. The current finding, that there is a large difference between the
use of negation in FRANTEXT and in the average Parisian play, invalidates
that assumption. And yet the fact remains that the Spread of Change study
found that the model developed by Lotka (1925) and Volterra (1926) fit
the FRANTEXT data. What are the implications of this for the validity of
the Spread of Change study, for extending the Topicalization study
(Grieve-Smith 2000) and for future studies of historical syntax?

© The Author(s) 2019
A. Grieve-Smith, *Building a Representative Theater Corpus*,
https://doi.org/10.1007/978-3-030-32402-5_8

Whatever corpus we use, it will always require a layer of subjective interpretation for the results. It is possible that FRANTEXT follows the Lotka-Volterra model even if it is not representative of all Parisian plays, because it is representative of the elite literary canon. The results of the Spread of Change study would then suggest that for the purposes of the theory of analogical extension, elite literary plays in one period serve as the input for elite literary playwrights of the next period. This in turn would imply that in French theater, the elite literary genres are self-contained and norms are rigidly enforced.

Usage-based theories hypothesize that the dynamic of competition based on type frequency exists not just in elite literary genres but everywhere in language. Have we now found evidence for it in theater, outside of elite literary subgenres? Not in this study, unfortunately. The Spread of Change study measured the effect at the scale of centuries and found that the language of one century could predict the language of the following century. We may well see evidence of this effect at a level below that of centuries, but we are unlikely to find a measurable effect across a 15-year period.

Work is continuing on Part II of the Digital Parisian Stage (1816–1830), and the rest of the nineteenth century will follow after that. It should be possible to test the Lotka-Volterra model on the full century, and possibly on half a century. This is an open source project that will be valuable to anyone studying changes in nineteenth-century Parisian French. It may take years with one scholar working to OCR, clean and format the texts, but if other scholars contribute to the process, the data will be available sooner.

The initial sample and studies that will be described in this book are steps on the path to better understanding the history of the French language, and language change in general. They follow the work of Charles Bally (1921), the FRANTEXT teams (Imbs 1971), Beaumont Wicks (1950 et seq.), Anthony Lodge (1991) and many others in compiling French texts beyond the canon and identifying features in those texts that are not found in the canon. There are many potential future directions: enlarging the sample; extending it beyond the Napoleonic period; examining correlations with characteristics of the text such as author, subgenre, theater and publisher; examining and quantifying correlations with the genre, age and social class of the characters; studying other negation-related variables; studying variables that are not expected to correlate with social class.

The Digital Parisian Stage corpus uses the power of representative sampling, the hard work of Beaumont Wicks and the massive archives of Google Books and Gallica to give us a better understanding of the language of the theaters in Paris in the nineteenth century. The differences between the initial sample and contemporary plays in FRANTEXT suggest that once the Digital Parisian Stage covers a longer period it will provide more reliable tests for hypotheses in diachronic linguistics.

References

Bally, Charles. 1921. *Traité de Stylistique Francaise*. 2nd ed. Heidelberg: Carl Winter.

Grieve-Smith, Angus. 2000. *Topicalization and Word Order in Conversational French*. Southeast Conference on Linguistics.

———. 2009. *The Spread of Change in French Negation*. Ph.D. diss., University of New Mexico.

Imbs, Paul. 1971. *Trésor de la langue française*. Paris: CNRS.

Lodge, Anthony. 1991. Molière's Peasants and the Norms of Spoken French. *Neuphilologische Mitteilungen* 92: 485–499.

Lotka, Alfred J. 1925. *Elements of Physical Biology*. Baltimore: Williams and Wilkins.

Volterra, Vito. 1926. Fluctuations in the Abundance of a Species Considered Mathematically. *Nature* 118: 558–560.

Wicks, Charles Beaumont. 1950, 1953, 1961, 1967, 1979. *The Parisian Stage*. Tuscaloosa: University of Alabama.

Appendix A: Theatrical Texts in FRANTEXT, 1800–1815

Table A.1 List of theatrical texts in FRANTEXT (1800–1815), with authors and première dates

Wicks no.	Title	Author
582	Cœlina, ou l'enfant du mystère	Guilbert de Pixérécourt, René Charles
2021	La Mort de Henri Quatre, Roi de France	Legouvé, Gabriel
2330	Pinto, ou la Journée d'une conspiration	Népomucène Lemercier, Louis Jean
	Wallstein	Constant de Rebecque, Benjamin

Table A.2 Genre and theater of the four plays in the FRANTEXT corpus (1800–1815)

Title	Première date	Genre	Theater
Cœlina	16 fructidor an VIII	drame	Théâtre de l'Ambigu-Comique
La Mort de Henri IV	June 25, 1806	tragédie	Théâtre Français
Pinto	1 germinal an VIII	comédie héroïque	Théâtre Français
Wallstein	1809	tragédie	Closet

© The Author(s) 2019
A. Grieve-Smith, *Building a Representative Theater Corpus*,
https://doi.org/10.1007/978-3-030-32402-5

Table A.3 Token frequencies of declarative sentence negations in the four plays in the FRANTEXT corpus (1800–1815)

Title	ne *alone*	ne ... pas	ne ... point	*Total*
Cœlina	27	88	31	146
La Mort de Henri IV	37	46	11	94
Pinto	51	98	36	185
Wallstein	37	36	33	106

Table A.4 Token frequencies of left dislocation constructions in the four plays in the FRANTEXT corpus (1800–1815)

Title	CI	CT	Prep	Conjoined	CLLD	Dem	Total
Cœlina	4	2	0	1	7	0	14
La Mort de Henri IV	11	3	1	0	9	0	26
Pinto	15	8	2	1	13	1	38
Wallstein	11	6	0	1	12	0	37

Table A.5 Token frequencies of right dislocation constructions in the four plays in the FRANTEXT corpus (1800–1815)

Title	CI	CAT	Prep	Conjoined	CLRD	Dem	Total
Cœlina	1	5	1	0	3	4	11
La Mort de Henri IV	0	0	0	0	1	0	2
Pinto	0	14	0	3	0	1	17
Wallstein	0	0	0	0	1	0	1

Appendix B: Texts in Part I of the Digital Parisian Stage Corpus (1800–1815)

Table B.1 All texts in the 1% sample, with titles, authors, première dates and availability

Random rank	Wicks No.	Title	Première date	Author	Status
1	1229	le Grenadier de Louis XV, ou le Lendemain de Fontenoy	December 22, 1814	J.-B. Dubois	Available
2	1563	Jocrisse maître et Jocrisse valet	October 29, 1810	Sewrin	Available
3	1291	les Héritiers Michau, ou le Moulin de Lieursain	April 30, 1814	Planard	Available
4	125	un An de Périclès	January 1, 1810	J. Aude	Available
5	1178	Gallet, ou le Chansonnier droguiste	November 22, 1806	Moreau & d'Allarde	Available
6	2050	Nephtali, ou les Ammonites	April 15, 1806	E. Aignan	Available
7	2025	la Mort du Capitaine Cook, ou les Insulaires d'O-why-e	October 13, 1814	Franconi	Available

(*continued*)

© The Author(s) 2019
A. Grieve-Smith, *Building a Representative Theater Corpus*,
https://doi.org/10.1007/978-3-030-32402-5

Table B.1 (continued)

Random rank	Wicks No.	Title	Première date	Author	Status
8	2701	le Singulier mariage	24 nivôse an IX	B. Dupont de Lille	Available
9	1903	la Méprise	November 22, 1815	Mme de Bawr	Not found
10	942	Esope chez Xantus	4 vendémiaire an IX	Tarenne de Laval	Available
11	926	l'Epreuve excusable	20 thermidor an VIII	Leroi de Neufvillette	Not found
12	2761	les Strélitz	May 12, 1808	Duperche & von Bilderbeck	Available
13	23	les Acteurs à l'épreuve	July 6, 1808	Sewrin & Chazet	Available
14	534	la Chaumière au pied des Alpes	May 4, 1810	Maillard, Brazier & Hapdé	Available
15	1127	Fontenelle	15 brumaire an XI	P.A.S. Petit aîné & Servières	Available
16	1544	la Jeunesse de Favart	February 11, 1808	A.-P.-C. Favart & Gentil de Chavagnac	Available
17	2576	le Rival obligeant	May 7, 1803	Mme de Bawr	Available
18	609a	le Compère futaille	February 18, 1803		Not found
19	1935	les Mœurs du jour, ou l'Ecole des jeunes femmes	7 thermidor an VIII	Collin d'Harleville	Available
20	371	la Bonne maîtresse, ou la Lettre trouvée	18 messidor an XI	Mme de Montanclos	Available
21	2861	les Trois Damis	January 4, 1804		Not found
22	259	Avis aux jaloux, ou la Rencontre imprévue	September 26, 1809	Chazet & Ourry	Available
23	2289	les Petits braconniers, ou les Ecoliers en vacances	April 5, 1813	Merle, Brazier & Charles Rondeau	Available
24	675	la Dame invisible	18 germinal an VIII	Chateauvieux, Armand Croizette & Fleureau de Ligny	Not found
25	279	le Baron de Felsheim	March 26, 1805	Beaunoir	Not found

(*continued*)

Table B.1 (continued)

Random rank	Wicks No.	Title	Première date	Author	Status
26	2065	Nitouche et Guignolet	17 nivôse an X	Dorvigny	Available
27	2838	les Tracasseries, ou M. et Mme Tatillon	June 25, 1804	Picard	Available
28	12	l'Absinthe	January 14, 1805	Ch. Henrion	Available
29	5	l'Abbaye de Grasville, ou le fantôme imaginaire	February 19, 1804	Boirie et Clément	Not found
30	2341	Plus de peur que de mal	August 28, 1803		Not found
31	2169	Papirius, ou les Femmes comme elles étaient	11 messidor an IX	Gersin & Vieillard	Available

Table B.2 Genres and theaters of the available plays in the Digital Parisian Stage corpus

Wicks no.	Title	Genre	Theater
1229	le Grenadier de Louis XV	comédie	Théâtre de la Gaîté
1563	Jocrisse maître et Jocrisse valet	comédie	Théâtre Montansier-Variétés
1291	les Héritiers Michau	opéra-comique	Opéra-Comique
125	un An de Périclès	prologue	Jeux Gymniques
1178	Gallet	comédie	Théâtre Montansier-Variétés
2050	Nephtali	opéra	Académie Impériale de Musique
2025	la Mort du Capitaine Cook	pantomime	Cirque Olympique
2701	le Singulier marriage	vaudeville	Théâtre des Jeunes Artistes
1903	la Méprise	comédie	Théâtre Français
942	Esope chez Xantus	comédie-vaudeville	Théâtre du Vaudeville
926	l'Epreuve excusable	comédie	Théâtre de la Gaîté
2761	les Strélitz	mélodrame	Théâtre de l'Ambigu-Comique
23	les Acteurs à l'épreuve	vaudeville	Théâtre Montansier-Variétés
534	la Chaumière au pied des Alpes	prologue	Jeux Gymniques

(*continued*)

Table B.2   (continued)

Wicks no.	Title	Genre	Theater
1127	Fontenelle	vaudeville	Théâtre des Jeunes Artistes
1544	la Jeunesse de Favart	comédie-vaudeville	Théâtre du Vaudeville
2576	le Rival obligeant	comédie	Théâtre de l'Ambigu-Comique
609a	le Compère futaille	vaudeville	Théâtre du Marais
1935	les Mœurs du jour	comédie	Théâtre Français
371	la Bonne maîtresse	comédie	Théâtre des Jeunes Artistes
2861	les Trois Damis		Théâtre de la Société Olympique
259	Avis aux jaloux	opéra-comique	Opéra-Comique
2289	les Petits braconniers	parade	Théâtre Montansier-Variétés
675	la Dame invisible	vaudeville	Théâtre Montansier-Variétés
279	le Baron de Felsheim	mélodrame-comique	Théâtre de la Porte-Saint-Martin
2065	Nitouche et Guignolet	comédie	Théâtre Montansier-Variétés
2838	les Tracasseries	comédie	Théâtre de l'Odéon
12	l'Absinthe	comédie	Théâtre des Nouveaux Troubadours
5	l'Abbaye de Grasville	mélodrame	Théâtre de la Gaîté
2341	Plus de peur que de mal		Théâtre du Marais
2169	Papirius	parade	Théâtre du Vaudeville

Table B.3   Token frequency of declarative sentence negation constructions in each available play in the Digital Parisian Stage corpus

Wicks no.	Title	ne *alone*	ne … pas	ne … point	Total negations
1229	le Grenadier de Louis XV	6	51	1	58
1563	Jocrisse maître et Jocrisse valet	8	63	7	78
1291	les Héritiers Michau	2	21	0	23
125	un An de Périclès	0	1	2	3
1178	Gallet	7	89	5	101
2050	Nephtali	8	3	2	13
2701	le Singulier mariage	15	50	34	99
942	Esope chez Xantus	11	72	6	89
2761	les Strélitz	25	24	30	79
23	les Acteurs à l'épreuve	8	37	3	48
534	la Chaumière au pied des Alpes	4	21	0	25

(*continued*)

Table B.3 (continued)

Wicks no.	Title	ne *alone*	ne ... pas	ne ... point	Total negations
1127	Fontenelle	9	56	8	73
1544	la Jeunesse de Favart	11	42	2	55
2576	le Rival obligeant	14	78	7	99
1935	les Mœurs du jour	53	105	48	206
371	la Bonne maîtresse	10	59	11	80
259	Avis aux jaloux	3	35	0	38
2289	les Petits braconniers	2	48	0	50
2065	Nitouche et Guignolet	11	73	1	85
2838	les Tracasseries	13	189	8	210
12	l'Absinthe	2	27	3	32
2169	Papirius	12	38	5	55

Table B.4 Token frequencies of left dislocation constructions in each available play of the Digital Parisian Stage corpus

Wicks no.	Title	CI	CT	Prep	Conjoined	CLLD	Dem	Total
1229	le Grenadier de Louis XV	0	3	0	0	2	3	8
1563	Jocrisse maître et Jocrisse valet	0	7	0	0	4	2	12
1291	les Héritiers Michau	1	2	0	0	3	0	6
125	un An de Périclès	3	0	0	0	0	0	3
1178	Gallet	1	9	1	0	5	0	15
2050	Nephtali	2	1	0	0	1	0	4
2701	le Singulier mariage	3	15	3	0	5	0	23
942	Esope chez Xantus	4	9	5	0	5	1	19
2761	les Strélitz	15	3	0	1	2	0	21
23	les Acteurs à l'épreuve	1	7	0	0	4	0	12
534	la Chaumière au pied des Alpes	2	0	0	0	0	0	2
1127	Fontenelle	7		1	0	5	1	12
1544	la Jeunesse de Favart	10	3	0	0	14	2	27
2576	le Rival obligeant	6	4	2	1	12	0	23
1935	les Mœurs du jour	12	49	6	0	24	2	92
371	la Bonne maîtresse	7	9	0	2	3	4	22
259	Avis aux jaloux	3	4	0	0	1	0	8
2289	les Petits braconniers		4	0	0	1	0	5
2065	Nitouche et Guignolet		6	1	0	2	1	9
2838	les Tracasseries	11	21	6	0	21	2	53
12	l'Absinthe	3	3	1	0	4	0	10
2169	Papirius	1	2	0	0	1	1	5

Table B.5 Token frequencies of right dislocation constructions in each available play of the Digital Parisian Stage corpus

Wicks no.	Title	CI	CAT	Prep	Conjoined	CLRD	Dem	Total
1229	le Grenadier de Louis XV	0	0	0	0	2	0	2
1563	Jocrisse maître et Jocrisse valet	0	17	0	0	6	3	23
1291	les Héritiers Michau	0	6	0	0	1	1	7
125	un An de Périclès	0	0	0	0	1	0	1
1178	Gallet	0	1	0	1	0	0	2
2050	Nephtali	0	0	0	0	2	0	2
2701	le Singulier mariage	0	0	0	0	5	0	5
942	Esope chez Xantus	0	2	0	0	1	0	3
2761	les Strélitz	0	0	0	0	6	0	6
23	les Acteurs à l'épreuve	0	3	0	0	0	0	3
534	la Chaumière au pied des Alpes	0	0	0	0	2	0	2
1127	Fontenelle	0	0	0	0	1	0	1
1544	la Jeunesse de Favart	1	2	0	0	2	0	5
2576	le Rival obligeant	0	6	1	0	4	2	11
1935	les Mœurs du jour	0	3	0	2	7	1	20
371	la Bonne maîtresse	0	4	1	1	7	2	12
259	Avis aux jaloux	0	0	0	0	1	0	1
2289	les Petits braconniers	1	2	0	0	2	2	5
2065	Nitouche et Guignolet	0	15	0	0	4	2	21
2838	les Tracasseries	1	3	0	0	11	3	18
12	l'Absinthe	0	0	0	0	1	0	1
2169	Papirius	0	0	0	0	1	0	1

Table B.6 The most frequent character, with social class, age and gender, in each available play in the Digital Parisian Stage corpus

Wicks no.	Title	Character	Class	Age	Gender
1229	le Grenadier de Louis XV	Francœur	Propriétaire	Adult	Man
1563	Jocrisse maître et Jocrisse valet	Jocrisse-Maître	Doméstique	Young adult	Man
1291	les Héritiers Michau	Suzette	Propriétaire	Young adult	Woman
125	un An de Périclès	Méonidas	Noble	Adult	Man
1178	Gallet	Piron	Bourgeois	Young adult	Man
2050	Nephtali	Nephtali	Noble	Adult	Man
2701	le Singulier mariage	Maurice	Paysan	Young adult	Man
942	Esope chez Xantus	Esope	Doméstique	Adult	Man
2761	les Strélitz	Maria	Noble	Elderly	Woman
23	les Acteurs à l'épreuve	Dupré	Bourgeois	Adult	Man

(*continued*)

Table B.6 (continued)

Wicks no.	Title	Character	Class	Age	Gender
534	la Chaumière au pied des Alpes	Zimeline	Paysan	Young adult	Woman
1127	Fontenelle	Fontenelle	Bourgeois	Adult	Man
1544	la Jeunesse de Favart	Charles	Bourgeois	Young adult	Man
2576	le Rival obligeant	Sainville	Bourgeois	Young adult	Man
1935	les Mœurs du jour	Formont	Propriétaire	Adult	Man
371	la Bonne maîtresse	Jacques	Domestique	Young adult	Man
259	Avis aux jaloux	Lorenzo	Noble	Elderly	Man
2289	les Petits braconniers	Félix	Noble	Teen	Man
2065	Nitouche et Guignolet	Guignolet	Paysan	Young adult	Man
2838	les Tracasseries	M. Tatillon	Propriétaire	Adult	Man
12	l'Absinthe	Hortence	Bourgeois	Elderly	Woman
2169	Papirius	Calphurnie	Noble	Adult	Woman

Table B.7 Token frequency of declarative sentence negation constructions for the most frequent character in each play of the Digital Parisian Stage corpus

Wicks no.	Title	Character	ne alone	ne ... pas	ne ... point	Total negations
1229	le Grenadier de Louis XV	Francœur	6	51	1	58
1563	Jocrisse maître et Jocrisse valet	Jocrisse-Maître	8	63	7	78
1291	les Héritiers Michau	Suzette	2	21	0	23
125	un An de Périclès	Méonidas	0	1	2	3
1178	Gallet	Piron	7	89	5	101
2050	Nephtali	Nephtali	8	3	2	13
2701	le Singulier mariage	Maurice	15	50	34	99
942	Esope chez Xantus	Esope	11	72	6	89
2761	les Strélitz	Maria	25	24	30	79
23	les Acteurs à l'épreuve	Dupré	8	37	3	48
534	la Chaumière au pied des Alpes	Zimeline	4	21	0	25
1127	Fontenelle	Fontenelle	9	56	8	73
1544	la Jeunesse de Favart	Charles	11	42	2	55
2576	le Rival obligeant	Sainville	14	78	7	99
1935	les Mœurs du jour	Formont	53	105	48	206
371	la Bonne maîtresse	Jacques	10	59	11	80
259	Avis aux jaloux	Lorenzo	3	35	0	38
2289	les Petits braconniers	Félix	2	48	0	50
2065	Nitouche et Guignolet	Guignolet	11	73	1	85
2838	les Tracasseries	M. Tatillon	13	189	8	210
12	l'Absinthe	Hortence	2	27	3	32
2169	Papirius	Calphurnie	12	38	5	55

Table B.8   Token frequencies of left dislocation constructions for the most frequent character in each available play of the Digital Parisian Stage corpus

Wicks no.	Title	Character	CI	CT	Prep	Conj	CLLD	Dem	Total
1229	le Grenadier de Louis XV	Francœur	0	0	0	0	0	1	1
1563	Jocrisse maître et Jocrisse valet	Jocrisse-Maître	0	3	0	0	4	1	8
1291	les Héritiers Michau	Suzette	1	0	0	0	0	0	1
125	un An de Périclès	Méonidas	0	0	0	0	0	0	0
1178	Gallet	Piron	0	6	0	0	1	0	7
2050	Nephtali	Nephtali	0	0	0	0	0	0	0
2701	le Singulier mariage	Maurice	2	5	0	0	4	0	11
942	Esope chez Xantus	Esope	0	5	0	0	1	0	6
2761	les Strélitz	Maria	2	1	0	0	1	0	4
23	les Acteurs à l'épreuve	Dupré	1	1	0	0	3	0	5
534	la Chaumière au pied des Alpes	Zimeline	0	0	0	0	0	0	0
1127	Fontenelle	Fontenelle	1	0	0	0	0	0	1
1544	la Jeunesse de Favart	Charles	4	0	0	0	2	0	6
2576	le Rival obligeant	Sainville	0	2	0	0	4	0	6
1935	les Mœurs du jour	Formont	0	9	0	0	4	0	13
371	la Bonne maîtresse	Jacques	0	5	0	0	3	2	9
259	Avis aux jaloux	Lorenzo	0	0	0	0	0	0	0
2289	les Petits braconniers	Félix	0	2	0	0	1	0	3
2065	Nitouche et Guignolet	Guignolet	0	4	1	0	1	1	6
2838	les Tracasseries	M. Tatillon	3	3	0	0	6	1	12
12	l'Absinthe	Hortence	1	1	0	0	1	0	3
2169	Papirius	Calphurnie	0	1	0	0	0	0	1

Table B.9 Token frequencies of right dislocation constructions for the most frequent character in each available play of the Digital Parisian Stage corpus

Wicks no.	Title	Character	CI	CAT	Prep	Conj	CLRD	Dem	Total
1229	le Grenadier de Louis XV	Francœur	0	0	0	0	2	0	2
1563	Jocrisse maître et Jocrisse valet	Jocrisse-Maître	0	9	0	0	3	1	12
1291	les Héritiers Michau	Suzette	0	5	0	0	0	0	5
125	un An de Périclès	Méonidas	0	0	0	0	1	0	1
1178	Gallet	Piron	0	0	0	0	0	0	0
2050	Nephtali	Nephtali	0	0	0	0	0	0	0
2701	le Singulier mariage	Maurice	0	0	0	0	4	0	4
942	Esope chez Xantus	Esope	0	1	0	0	0	0	1
2761	les Strélitz	Maria	0	0	0	0	3	0	3
23	les Acteurs à l'épreuve	Dupré	0	1	0	0	0	0	1
534	la Chaumière au pied des Alpes	Zimeline	0	0	0	0	2	0	2
1127	Fontenelle	Fontenelle	0	0	0	0	0	0	0
1544	la Jeunesse de Favart	Charles	1	0	0	0	0	0	1
2576	le Rival obligeant	Sainville	0	6	0	0	2	2	9
1935	les Mœurs du jour	Formont	0	2	0	1	0	1	4
371	la Bonne maîtresse	Jacques	0	4	1	0	4	2	8
259	Avis aux jaloux	Lorenzo	0	0	0	0	0	0	0
2289	les Petits braconniers	Félix	0	0	0	0	0	0	0
2065	Nitouche et Guignolet	Guignolet	0	4	0	0	3	2	8
2838	les Tracasseries	M. Tatillon	0	1	0	0	3	2	6
12	l'Absinthe	Hortence	0	0	0	0	0	0	0
2169	Papirius	Calphurnie	0	0	0	0	1	0	1

GLOSSARY

Analogical extension A process of language change whereby language users create new forms by applying analogies to existing forms in their input.

Clitic dislocation A form of dislocation where the pronoun indicating the referent's role in the argument structure of the sentence is a clitic pronoun.

Conjoined noun phrase Two noun phrases joined with a coordinating conjunction like *et* "and" or *ou* "or." A dislocation-like structure, with a coreferential clitic pronoun, may be used to indicate the role of the referents in the argument structure of the sentence.

Contrastive antitopic A form of right dislocation where the dislocated constituent is an oblique pronoun like *moi* "me" or *vous* "you."

Contrastive topic A form of left dislocation where the dislocated constituent is an oblique pronoun like *moi* "me" or *vous* "you."

Demonstrative dislocation A form of dislocation where the pronoun indicating the role of the referent in the argument structure of the sentence is a demonstrative pronoun.

Left dislocation A construction with a noun phrase produced before a sentence, and a pronoun in that sentence that has the same referent as the dislocated noun phrase, indicating the role of the referent in the argument structure of the sentence.

Predicate negation An unmarked construction indicating that a predicate is negated.

© The Author(s) 2019

A. Grieve-Smith, *Building a Representative Theater Corpus*,
https://doi.org/10.1007/978-3-030-32402-5

Presupposition denial A construction indicating that a likely presupposition of the conversation is not true.

Principle of Authority The method used by the French Centre national de la recherche scientifique (CNRS) to select texts for the *Trésor de la langue française* corpus, by counting the number of times a text was mentioned by literary historians.

Representative corpus A corpus based on a representative sample.

Right dislocation A construction with a noun phrase produced after a sentence, and a pronoun in that sentence that is coreferential with that dislocated noun phrase.

Sampling error The possibility that the items selected for the sample are not representative of the sampling frame.

Sampling frame A comprehensive list of objects of interest to be used for a representative sample.

Token frequency The number of tokens of a linguistic form in a text, usually as a fraction of the number of words in that text.

Type frequency The number of distinct linguistic forms that co-occur with a given construction, relative to that construction's alternatives in the envelope of variation.

Usage-based linguistics Theories that explain or predict forms of language as a function of prior usage.

Index

© The Author(s) 2019
A. Grieve-Smith, *Building a Representative Theater Corpus*,
https://doi.org/10.1007/978-3-030-32402-5

GPSR Compliance
The European Union's (EU) General Product Safety Regulation (GPSR) is a set
of rules that requires consumer products to be safe and our obligations to
ensure this.

If you have any concerns about our products, you can contact us on

ProductSafety@springernature.com

In case Publisher is established outside the EU, the EU authorized
representative is:

Springer Nature Customer Service Center GmbH
Europaplatz 3
69115 Heidelberg, Germany

www.ingramcontent.com/pod-product-compliance
Lightning Source LLC
LaVergne TN
LVHW011754070326
832904LV00034B/291

* 9 7 8 3 0 3 0 3 2 4 0 1 8 *